Updating
CLASSIC AMERICA
CAPES

Updating
CLASSIC AMERICA
CAPES

Design Ideas
for Renovating,
Remodeling, and
Building New

Jane Gitlin

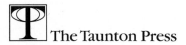

The Taunton Press

The Taunton Press
Inspiration for hands-on living™

The Taunton Press, Inc., 63 South Main Street, PO Box 5506, Newtown, CT 06470-5506
e-mail: tp@taunton.com

Distributed by Publishers Group West

EDITOR: Roger Yepsen
DESIGN AND LAYOUT: Lori Wendin
ILLUSTRATOR: Christine Erikson

LIBRARY OF CONGRESS CATALOGING-IN-PUBLICATION DATA:

Gitlin, Jane.
    Capes : design ideas for renovating, remodeling, and building new /
Jane Gitlin.
        p. cm. — (Updating classic America)
Includes index.
    ISBN 1-56158-436-3
    1. Cape Cod houses. 2. Architecture, Domestic—United States. I.
Title: Design ideas for renovating, remodeling, and building new. II.
Title. III. Series

    NA7205 .G52 2003
    728'.37'0973—dc21

                            2002151663

Printed in Singapore
10 9 8 7 6 5 4 3 2 1

For Michael, Mack,
and David

Acknowledgments

I AM GRATEFUL TO MANY PEOPLE who offered good-humored and valuable assistance during the process of researching, writing, composing, and producing this volume. Completing this book turned out to be a lot like a construction project, starting with a budget, a schedule, a team, and the big ideas sketched out. Through many outlines, drafts, and reams of paper, this book was slowly built—composed from great hunks of text that were written out of sequence and then gradually organized on paper.

For research materials, special illustrations, and historic information I am indebted to Richard Wills of Royal Barry Wills Architects; Ann Glorioso, librarian at the Levittown (New York) Public Library; Stanley Schuler; Peter Strauss; Barry Hammons; Robert Braun; and Steve Culpepper. I am obliged to all the homeowners and architects who submitted their Capes. Thank you for graciously supplying plans, snapshots, and stories and especially for allowing perfect strangers into your homes. These houses are shown to their best advantage through the work of photographers Richard Bienkowski, Ken Gutmaker, Chipper Hatter, David Livingston, and Randy O'Rourke.

Thank you to the staff at The Taunton Press for this opportunity and for your solid support and valuable guidance. In particular, I am beholden to Peter Chapman, for guiding the project; to Carol Kasper, Stefanie Ramp, Jennifer Renjilian Morris, Carolyn Mandarano, Candace Levy, Carol Singer, and Robyn Doyon-Aitken, for making sure things got done properly; and to Wendi Mijal and Paula Schlosser, for creating a beautiful product. I owe a debt of gratitude to wordsmith, editor, and pen pal Roger Yepsen for his insightful criticism, succinct editing, and the occasional prodding.

Heartfelt thanks to the many friends who egged me on and provided motivation, technical support, meals, and opinions, especially my colleagues at Z: Architecture: Matthew Schoenherr, Kevin Huelster, Charles Emerson, Vawn Edele, Giancarlo Massaro, and Sally Enos. Thanks also to Robert Gerloff, Kristina Boland, Amy Mezoff, Lynne Porter, Jennifer Braun, Carrie Pittu, Michael Ferguson, Tanya Gillette, Rob Young, and my Middlebrook neighbors.

And thank you, of course, to my loving family, David, Mack, and Michael Nishball, who make our Connecticut Cape, "Happy Site," our home.

CONTENTS

Introduction 2

CHAPTER ONE An American Archetype 4

The Cape Makes a Comeback 6
Updating a Classic Cape 10
A Contemporary Twist on Tradition 10
Moving toward the Light 14
The Hallmarks of Cape Style 18
Cape Renaissance 25
Choosing a Strategy 30

CHAPTER TWO Modest Remodels 34

Big Plans for a Small Area 36
Modernizing at the Core 37
Working with What You've Got 40
Modest Isn't Mundane 42
Underfoot and Overhead 44
When Dowdy Won't Do 46
Room at the Top 52

Instant Tradition 60
Southern Comfort 70
Perfectly Architectural 78

CHAPTER THREE Ambitious Additions 86

A Marriage of New and Old 88
Stretching Out and Up 92
The Morphed Cape 95
Opening a Cape to the Outdoors 98
From Cape to Colonial 102
From Cape to Bungalow 108
A Spirited Transformation 116
Trial Size to Family Size 124
A Cape Compound 132
A Cape for the Generations 138
Stone Sprawler 148

CHAPTER FOUR New Homes from an Old Pattern 158

An Architecture of Substance 160
Cape Shape 162
The Benefit of a Budget 168
Little "*a*" Architecture 176
A Cape with a New Twist 182
A Cape Reborn 190
To the Edge and Back 198

CHAPTER FIVE New Directions 206

In the Image of a Cape 208
Upside-Down Cape 212
The Essence of Home 214

Sources 216
Index 218

INTRODUCTION

WHEN OUR FAMILY RENOVATED A POST-war Cape a couple of years ago, we removed the drywall in one room to discover a yellowed 1947 newspaper that had been tucked between the studs. No doubt some carpenter had thought of the paper as a time capsule of sorts. I don't know that he expected it to be uncovered just 50-odd years later. It seems most of us think that our homes are eternal, that their style won't ever seem dowdy, that their roofs will stay straight and true.

We Cape owners, especially, can be excused for thinking of our houses as permanent parts of the land-

scape. After all, Cape Cod–style homes have been around nearly forever. Their simple one-and-a-half-story form remains a part of our architectural vocabulary—even though most Capes were built within the last century and their construction and room functions have changed dramatically. If Mayflower Puritans were to visit a new Cape Cod–style house, whether in Massachusetts or in California, chances are they would find it comfortingly familiar.

As the renovations proceeded on our own Cape and it was time to resheathe the rooms with new drywall, we returned the 1947 newspaper to its niche and added a current issue. Reluctantly, we had to acknowledge that no matter how splendid our modifications seem right now, only 50 years or so will pass before another family feels the need to breathe new life into this home. The Cape style lends itself to being reinvented, which is one of the main reasons for its remarkable longevity.

Like a dish of vanilla ice cream, a Cape gracefully accepts just about any flavor you might want to add. The homes in this book illustrate many ways in which the basic form has been embellished, stretched, and altered. I hope these examples will inspire you to craft a Cape that goes beyond the ordinary, in both its beauty and in its function.

CHAPTER ONE

AN AMERICAN ARCHETYPE

ABOVE, **This recently built** vacation home features all the traditional hallmarks of the Cape style—prominent chimney, modest aspect, multipaned windows, and dormers above.

FACING PAGE, **The Cape Cod house** has endured since the 1600s and is an icon of the humble home on the American architectural landscape.

NEXT TIME YOU PLAY MONOPOLY, TAKE A GOOD look at the little green houses that you rack up on Marvin Gardens. If you put your head down for a bug's-eye view, you will see a pretty good representation of the ubiquitous Cape Cod house, found in almost every suburb in the country. Yes, these little plastic pieces seem like a cartoon of a house— more like an icon on your computer screen—but they are a fair model of the Cape style.

Capes are found in towns, suburbs, and rural areas alike. There are colonial-era Capes, and Capes that are under construction right now; but the vast majority were built in the couple of decades following World War II. The term *Cape Cod style* is tossed around a lot, and it has several connotations. To an architect like myself, a Cape is a story-and-a-half dwelling with a steeply pitched roof. To a real estate agent, it's almost any small house with a certain New England look, particularly if it is capped by a number of dormers. To a

This classic "Half Cape" was built close to the shore in the 1960s. New shingle siding and trim tie the original building into the new addition, which was added 35 years later.

Simple, primary colors can do a lot to jazz up a Cape interior. Red, white, and blue are a world away from the ivory, beige, and avocado of most kitchens, and they add spice to this somewhat low space.

developer, a Cape might be a less-than-profitable project in this era of conspicuous consumption.

And to you, a potential buyer? You may discover in the Cape a straightforward style that combines a characteristic Yankee practicality with a timeless aesthetic. And a particular Cape, new or renewed, might be the home of your dreams.

The Cape Makes a Comeback

Capes and their neighborhoods are enjoying a renaissance. That's true in spite of the current widespread practice of trading up to houses that shout dollars rather than sense. It seems a new generation of homeowners is attracted to Capes for reasons that are both emotional and economic.

On the emotional side, a Cape tends to be seen as a cozy cottage with a smiling facade, shutters, and smoke tendrils curling out of the chimney. Or a Cape might

This new California house stretches the notion of what a Cape can be, with informal areas open to each other and easy access to the terrace outside.

be a memory of a summer's cheerful seaside home, to which the family returned for dinner after a day of seafaring or sunbathing. And for others, it's the familiar image of the suburban home, with a basketball hoop on the garage, a barbecue grill out back, and fireflies winking in the yard.

A more practical reason for the Cape's comeback is the affordability of a relatively small house on a modest lot. A Cape costs considerably less than the average new house—and average construction costs continue to rise. Beyond the appeal of the structure itself, these houses often line the streets of established neighborhoods where folks really act like neighbors. They tend to be found in communities with sidewalks, mature trees, and a short ride to stores and the library. By moving into a Cape, chances are you also are buying into a piece of the neighborhood quilt.

The Cape Springs Eternal

FOR MANY AMERICANS, the Cape is the essence of house. Its bloodlines are as obvious as those of a pedigreed show dog. Here is an informal view of Massachusetts Capes in roughly the middle of their lifespan: Reverend Timothy Dwight is describing the houses he saw while traveling in 1882.

"The houses in Yarmouth are inferiour to those in Barnstable, and much more generally of the class, which may be called, with propriety, Cape Cod houses. These have one story, and four rooms on the lower floor; and are covered on the sides, as well as the roofs, with pine shingles, eighteen inches in length. The chimney is in the middle, imme-

diately behind the front door; and on each side of the door are two windows. The roof is straight. Under it are two chambers; and there are two larger, and two smaller, windows in the gable end.... A great proportion of them are in good repair. Generally, they exhibit a tidy, neat aspect in themselves, and in their appendages; and furnish proofs of comfortable living, by which I was at once disappointed, and gratified."

You are apt to find these suburbs to be agreeably inclusive. In my Connecticut neighborhood, not only are there the typical American families with two parents, a couple of kids, and a dog but there are also single-parent families, couples of all persuasions, older couples with grown children, and single adults. Young families have moved here after having outgrown their apartments. Others want homes within convenient commuting distance of their downtown jobs. Some are happily inheriting their parents' homes. And empty-nesters want to downsize to a modest Cape as an alternative to a condominium or apartment.

The urge for a tangible sense of home is particularly strong today, because many of us spend such long hours preoccupied with our work. The Cape, in its characteristic neighborhood, fulfills the need for a comfortable nest to return to at the end of the day. But like many a 50-year-old, these structures tend to need some work. A face-lift, a makeover, or a major addition—this book suggests the ways in which you can update a Cape and prepare it for the century ahead, in a way that is consistent with your household's particular needs.

This Cape was expanded by adding a gambrel roof, a wrinkle on the conventional gable roof that creates more headroom and more usable floor area. The gambrel design also spares resources by using shorter lengths of wood for its framing.

Updating a Classic Cape

When Dale and Hillary searched for a weekend retreat, they weren't expecting to find a house exactly to their liking. Their top priorities were the familiar real estate triad of location, location, and location—a house can be altered more easily than its surroundings after all. When they purchased a bland postwar Cape near the shore in Fairfield County, Connecticut, they were delighted by the quiet street and the short stroll to the neighborhood association's own beach on Long Island Sound. The house wasn't in bad shape, and what it lacked in personality it had in potential.

The couple described their must-have requirements to architect Robert Cardello: a playroom for their kids, an open and informal plan, and a terrace out back for summer evenings. Along the way, they hoped for architectural detailing that would spice up the otherwise ordinary Cape trim. The couple wanted a jewel box rather than the largest vinyl-clad box their budget could tolerate.

A Contemporary Twist on Tradition

All too often in smaller homes, the transitional spaces go neglected. These are the parts of a house that link one area with another—front stoops, entryways, and halls. When space is limited, they tend to be overlooked in favor of investing more square feet in identifiable rooms. And not without reason—we've all visited houses that seem full of dead ends and redundant halls.

But if you think about all the activities that take place in these in-between areas, you can appreciate that they are difficult to dispense with altogether. The front stoop is the spot for a goodnight kiss or waiting for the school bus on a rainy day. Entryways are suited to a display of family pictures and a table on which to drop the car keys and mail. Halls can both direct traffic efficiently

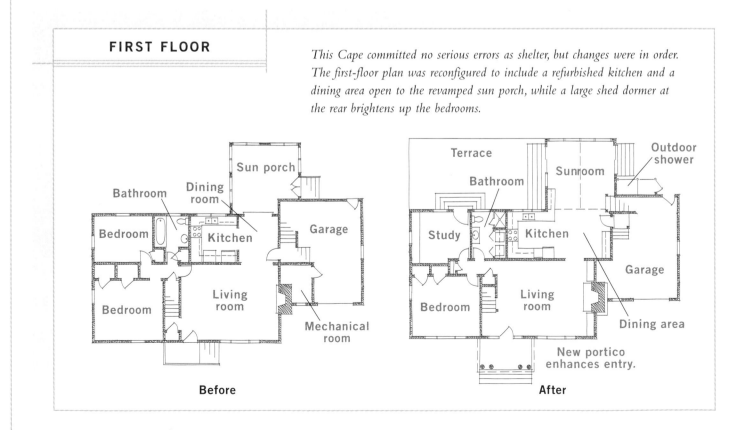

FIRST FLOOR

This Cape committed no serious errors as shelter, but changes were in order. The first-floor plan was reconfigured to include a refurbished kitchen and a dining area open to the revamped sun porch, while a large shed dormer at the rear brightens up the bedrooms.

Sun porch · Bathroom · Dining room · Bedroom · Kitchen · Garage · Bedroom · Living room · Mechanical room

Before

Terrace · Outdoor shower · Bathroom · Sunroom · Study · Kitchen · Bedroom · Living room · Garage · Dining area · New portico enhances entry.

After

Windows and doors can be used as spices to perk up the bland stew of an exterior. They should not be added heedlessly, but with some thought to a similar style and the way in which they are aligned on a facade.

Kitchens are no longer the hidden laboratories of earlier generations. The granite-topped counters of this home snake around to the perimeter of a living area, blurring the distinction between kitchen work and family play.

portico —A covered entrance to the home.

ridge —The highest edge of a gable roof, where the sloped planes meet.

and, if wide and inviting enough, provide semiprivate places to read, chat, or play. And as shown throughout this book, a house can be brought above the ordinary by the attention paid to the portals and passageways between its rooms.

Architect Robert Cardello focused on these connections. He began by designing a graciously sized and formally detailed **portico.** This feature adds a bit of ceremony to what had been a severely plain front elevation. It also compensates for the fact that Dale and Hillary had not planned on adding a front hall. Entering the house, you immediately find yourself at the foot of the stairway, which is the usual introduction to a Cape household. This arrangement may not be elegant but it makes practical sense, allowing the top of the stair to reach the second floor under the roof's **ridge,** where headroom is at its modest maximum.

As in many Capes, the living room needed help to escape its narrow role as a formal gathering spot. Bookcases and cabinets were built in to either side of the fireplace, making the room seem more intimate and inviting. With a wide opening to the dining room and the sunroom in view, the living room no longer feels isolated from the vital activity of the home.

In line with the contemporary trend, the Cape's 1950s kitchen was converted from a utility room for food prep into a bright, open space. The room's generous size, handsome cabinets, and stone counters help establish its role as the new heart of this home. There is just one table for dining, a good space-saving approach for small houses. Because the kitchen is open to the rest of the house, it draws the family for socializing as well as for snacking. The room seems more like living space than a work area, thanks to its uncluttered look, understated appliances, and wood floors.

In a small house, you create an impression of space by planning long views from one room to another. An easy way of doing this is to widen the openings between rooms, so that they seem to contribute to one another while maintaining their identity.

Moving toward the Light

If the kitchen is the core of this modernized Cape, the new sunroom has become its focal point. This former porch is surrounded on three sides by a carefully composed selection of windows, as handsome from outside as from within. The windows contribute all the more to the room because of their broad, confident trim. The space is open to the soaring ceiling, which is clad in **beadboard** rather than the drywall used elsewhere. The ceiling can do a lot to establish the function of a room. A tall, bright space invites social gatherings, while a room with lower ceilings, like the living room in this home, will seem right for quieter pastimes.

Back when most Capes were built, children's particular needs weren't considered very seriously. Times have changed, and this house has a playroom placed in a prime location, in its own world above the garage. Tucked under a broad shed dormer, this is a haven where children and their toys won't be underfoot, while allowing the grownups to stay within earshot. Later, the room can become a teen's territory with just the right degree of privacy.

The back of the house originally had a standard-issue full-shed dormer, which provided plenty of space but no architectural flair whatsoever. It was replaced with an unusual version of a Nantucket dormer, a three-in-one structure that links a pair of earlike gable dormers with a shed dormer (see the photo on p. 17). Around front, conventional gable dormers sit on either side of the new entry. They are flared just slightly at the base, matching the subtle "kick" at the lower edge of the home's main roof. While just about everything on a

beadboard Strips of wood with an ornamental bead, usually run vertically, used to sheathe entire walls, for wainscoting, and for ceilings.

Multiple child-size casement windows set the playful tone for this kid-friendly room, just a short flight of stairs from the family spaces.

typical Cape could be drawn with a ruler, these details add ever-so-slight sensual curves.

On the inside, the gable dormers frame intimate alcoves in the front bedrooms that are just the right size for a desk or bureau. A mix of dormers ensures that the upstairs will have the quirky volumes that distinguish the second floor of so many Capes.

There is nothing particularly interesting about the usual postwar Cape's window formula: double-hung units, two to a room, with the living room treated to the

The glossy white beadboard ceilings of the sunroom follow the slope of the rafters. A high ceiling like this on the inside allows the architect to specify a tall, dramatic window that makes a bold statement on the outside.

ABOVE, **In many successful remodelings,** the Cape presents a sober side to the street and loosens up around back. The private facade of this home combines the grand window treatment of the sunroom on the right with the whimsy of the copious playroom casements.

FACING PAGE, **Following the lines of the house,** this terrace serves as outdoor room. Capes often are set low to the ground, which allows building outside features that draw less attention to themselves than an elevated deck.

Cyclops eye of a picture window. To bring more life to this home, Robert specified a medley of **awning**, double-hung, and **casement** windows, as well as French doors. The sunroom's curvy transom, surrounded by a white paneled effect, draws the eye in the same way that this space does on the inside. To make sure that all of the variety doesn't seem too busy, each window is divided by traditional muntins.

Through it all, this Cape unabashedly remained a Cape. There was no attempt to morph its New England style into another, nor was Robert given the mission to bump this second home up to the level of luxury. The renovation was a success, given that Hillary and Dale now find themselves drawn to the house for more than just weekends, and they look forward to moving there year-round some day.

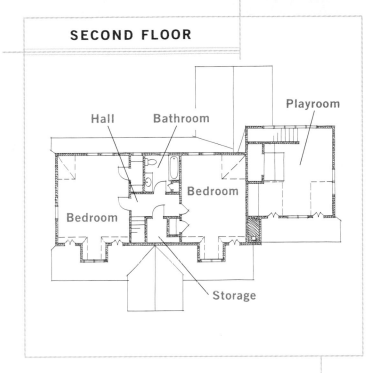

SECOND FLOOR

Playroom

Hall   Bathroom

Bedroom

Bedroom

Storage

awning —A window that hinges from the top of the frame.

casement —A window that hinges along a side of the frame.

The Peck House in Old Lyme, Connecticut, purportedly built in 1666, is one of the oldest surviving Capes. According to the current owner, it is haunted by some good-willed and generous spirits.

The Hallmarks of Cape Style

As you'll see with many of the Capes in this book, historically accurate details often have less impact than the overall design. Unless you are determined to create an exact replica of a particular vintage, feel free to tamper with tradition, mixing and matching elements that appeal to you. Nevertheless, to come up with a pleasing and coherent plan, it's worthwhile to be familiar with the hallmarks of the Cape style.

Much like the Capes in the first postwar subdivisions, the earliest colonial Capes were built as starter homes. This allowed the maximum number of families to be housed with the minimum expenditure and resources. The first Capes were less about creating a charming cottage than they were about shelter—an improvement over huts hastily constructed from ships' sails and tree branches.

In *Cape Cod Architecture* (Parnassus, 1989), Claire Baisly gives the defining characteristics of the New England Cape. It was exclusively of wood and boxy in shape, with a steeply pitched roof and a massive chimney aligned with the front door. Among the signature details were small-paned windows, unapologetically plain trim, and shallow overhangs at the rake and the eaves. Although this list is short, Baisly points out that "Cape Cod architecture is not a simple formula that can be expressed by the number and placement of the doors and windows of the house facade, but an intricate, three-dimensional weaving of many factors that complicate architectural progression everywhere."

Although the earliest Massachusetts settlers had been accustomed to England's thatched wattle-and-daub cot-

Steep roofs and small multipaned windows are hallmarks of the Cape style, shown here in a contemporary interpretation.

The Essential Cape

HISTORIC CAPES were larger in size than the familiar postwar version, yet they share the same defining characteristics. Both are rectangular boxes with steep roofs. An old example is apt to have low eaves and ceilings just 7 ft. high, whereas modern Capes typically offer another 6 in. of headroom, in part because of the minimum stated by building codes.

Although the standard Cape gable roof makes a precipitous climb of between 8 in. and 12 in. to the foot (with 10 in. being the most common), variants include gambrel and bowed roofs. The houses traditionally are sided with shingles or clapboards, painted or left to weather to a distinctive gray; but Capes are also seen in brick, stucco, and stone. The style of windows does a lot to place a date on a house. Picture windows, ganged (side-by-side) windows, and full-length glass doors are

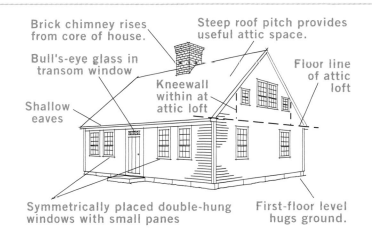

Brick chimney rises from core of house.

Steep roof pitch provides useful attic space.

Bull's-eye glass in transom window

Floor line of attic loft

Kneewall within at attic loft

Shallow eaves

Symmetrically placed double-hung windows with small panes

First-floor level hugs ground.

all relatively recent innovations and were never seen on Capes before the mid-1900s.

Despite their evolution over a period of 350 years, Capes have changed remarkably little from the outside. They remain America's first home of European origin and an enduring symbol of domestic comfort.

---

tages, they quickly shifted to building tight structures entirely of wood framing, siding, and roofing. The seemingly endless New England forest provided the materials, and the harsh climate provided the incentive. These homes did retain the traditional English heavy framing, but instead of mud and straw, the houses were clad with nonstructural wood planking topped by overlapping shingles. A roof of wood shingles was quicker to put up and hardier than thatch in severe weather.

The boxy shape has its practical value. It allows huddling several chambers around one or more fireplaces that share a common heat-conserving chimney. In the blustery New England climate, staying warm (and staying alive) was paramount, and the fireplace was the source of heat, light, and dinner. The hearth wasn't just a symbol of the home but its literal core.

The steep roof silhouette is another Cape hallmark, and again there are practical benefits. Rain and snow are quickly shed, and, more important, the pitch allows more standing room in the attic. Our *Mayflower* ancestors used the attic for storage and as the children's sleeping loft.

The small multipaned windows were symmetrically arranged around a centrally located front door. (If the house is a smaller "half" or "three-quarter" Cape, the door may be offset.) Glass was expensive and shipped over from England in small pieces, 6 in. by 8 in., to reduce breakage. Later on, flanking shutters were added to protect the windows and to give some measure of security as well.

Trim not only conceals the seams of the house but also has the aesthetic function of defining the edges of

Trim Talk

ON A CAPE, with its spare features, details matter. Exterior trim tends to look weak, cheap, and flimsy if it is very thin, especially around doors and windows. If you are replacing the trim on a wood-sided Cape, select a wider, flat exterior casing rather than brick molding; this narrow, curved trim was designed for brick and stucco homes.

A generous casing also provides a place from which to hang shutters in an authentic way. The trim around a front door is usually more extensive and may incorporate shutters, windows, and sidelights, with a small roof overhang to shelter the steps. Historic Capes often have transom windows with bull's-eye glass over the front door to let light into the vestibule.

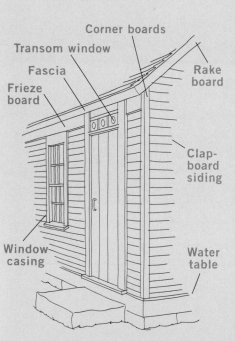

Rake boards, corner boards, fascias, water tables, and soffits are elements that frame and outline the edges of a house. If they are skimpy—or lacking altogether—the house seems to blur into the sky. They also can be overdone and gussied up, with the effect of weighing the house down.

things—windows and doors, roofs, and outside corners. In the earliest Capes, trim was spare, serving only as a seal where one surface met another. Over time, these strips of wood became slightly more elaborate, with particular emphasis around the front door. But in all Capes, the roof overhangs and the trim pieces marking them were minimal, with the express purpose of reducing the wind's grasp on the roof; the earliest Capes were built along the shore by seasoned 1600s craftsmen who had more than a little experience with harsh Atlantic winds.

Capes built within the past several decades retain many of these exterior details, even though modern building methods and materials have made some classic features completely vestigial. Houses don't follow a Darwinian model, because nostalgia and our love of things "old-timey" have preserved certain symbolic features. For example, houses now have central heating, so our fireplaces are just for enjoyment and the masonry chimneys simply give the house some architectural punctuation. Similarly, window and door shutters are no longer shut to keep out the bad weather (and the riffraff) but are applied as decoration.

A CLUSTER OF ROOMS

On a recent school field trip with my sons to the Ogden House, a 1600s Saltbox (the big sister of the modest Cape) here in Fairfield, Connecticut, I was struck by the similarities between it and our own 1947 Cape in a nearby neighborhood. Although the names of rooms have changed over the centuries, the activities remain much the same. In that historic house, the hall, parlor, and keeping room have evolved into our Cape's living room, dining room, and kitchen. Even the configuration and relative sizes of the rooms are similar.

The very first Capes weren't even that elaborate but existed as mean one-room shelters. Fireplace and hearth

This colorful family room overlooks the rear garden and is connected to the playroom below by a sun-filled stairway.

A broad shed dormer opens up a vista at the foot of the bed.

were at the center of the home and provided the heat essential for cooking and for surviving the severe New England winters. Families ate, slept, prayed, and played in the single room, referred to as the hall. Steep stairs alongside the chimney led to the attic.

Once families became established in their new location, a parlor with its own fireplace was added to the other side of the hall, creating one massive chimney running through the center of the house. The parlor was used for receiving guests and sleeping, and the original hall served for everything else. Then, as families grew, more room was added to the back of the house by continuing the rear roof pitch downward in the Saltbox style.

Or a new "deluxe" Cape was built with several ground-floor rooms grouped around the massive chimney, each with its own fireplace. It could be that our ancestors succumbed to the keeping-up-with-the-Joneses mentality in building bigger and bigger houses. The hall and the parlor were used for both the more ceremonial aspects of life (receiving guests, mourning) and the more intimate (sleeping, procreating). The large ground-floor space that ran behind the hall and parlor was called the kitchen, or keeping room, and it is the predecessor of the combined family room and kitchen we build today. It housed the practical business of life—weaving, cooking, manufacturing, sewing. Small closet-like rooms at either end of the keeping room were used as the pantry, buttery, and birthing rooms.

If you were to slice vertically through a Cape, you'd see cozy upstairs rooms tucked under the steep roof that is so essential to a Cape's identity. These shadowy attic spaces eventually were given dormers for better headroom and more natural light.

☆ Size Matters

cape pedigree

CAPES WERE THE FIRST "starter homes" in that they were planned and sized according to the owner's economic and social stature. As a family prospered and grew, the Cape was enlarged. Half Capes, which were built with the expectation of being completed later on, have their chimney at the side of the single chamber, so that it would end up in the center of the house when completed. Half Capes grew into Three-Quarter or Full Capes, and additions sprouted up to house more children, the spinster aunt, or a home-based business. In northern New England, the additions out the back would reach all the way to the barn so family members could avoid going outside in cold, wet weather.

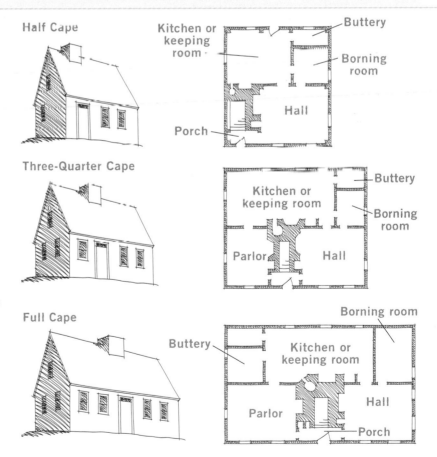

An American Archetype 23

Levittown's Legacy

THE CAPE DIDN'T BECOME a universal American style until after World War II. The first firm to produce them—or any style—on a grand scale was Levitt and Sons in Long Island, New York. During the war years, the Levitts' experience in producing war workers' housing taught them how to streamline the construction process to the point that homes could be built virtually overnight. In the first Levittown, within commuting distance to New York City, more than 17,000 houses were constructed between 1947 and 1950, making it the largest housing development ever built. The company went on to build two other Levittowns, in New Jersey and in Pennsylvania.

The Levitt Company founded its success on assembly-line principles: Build the most house for the least amount of money in the shortest possible time. Individuality was left up to the new homeowners.

Using a factory production line as a model, houses were manufactured as products rather than individually crafted. Roads and lots were staked out, trucks dropped off precut bundles of lumber at each lot, and specialized crews performed just one task at each house before moving on to the next. Houses sprung up at a terrific rate, peaking at 36 a day.

The houses were even marketed like manufactured products. Purchasing a house was rather like shopping for a car, in that buyers were presented with a few distinct models to select from. Amenities like washing machines and televisions were bundled into the purchase price, adding further incentive to buy. The Levittown sales package was so persuasive that, once on a single day, 1,400 sales contracts were drawn up.

The success of the Levitts prompted others to mass produce basic models, and housing developments quickly became a part of the American landscape.

In a Levittown development, curved streets create the now-familiar suburban atmosphere, in which there are few corner lots and each property is equal to its neighbor. Instead of selecting houses for their location, prospective buyers based their choice on color or design touches, something like shopping for a shirt.

Cape Renaissance

Traditional Capes continued to be built into the 1800s, but they were no longer the dominant style in the poshest communities. In fact, Capes were never really considered as being a particular style—they were just generic houses and as such fell below the radar of architectural history.

Boston architect Royal Barry Wills is credited with reintroducing Capes in the late 1920s as a suitable prototype for the contemporary small home. This was a departure, at a time when other young architects were either turning to the European Modern movement for inspiration or continuing to design houses with 1800s origins—Gothic, Victorian, Italianate, and Greek Revival had all been in vogue in the preceding 100 years.

A native of Massachusetts, Wills studied the historic Capes of the region and refined the style for a middle-class family's needs. He retained the essential Cape ingredients—the steeply pitched roof over a story-and-a-half structure, even though the floor plan within had changed. Rather than the traditional arrangement of a hall, parlor, and keeping room, Wills's Capes featured a living room, dining room, bathroom, and kitchen downstairs, and two bedrooms upstairs. And yet he retained the central chimney and stair, as well as the proportions and scale that imparted charm and sensibility to the historic model. In following his four tenets of design—suitability, utility, beauty, and economy—Wills carefully detailed his houses, inside and out, to feature the craftsmanship of the old with the modern conveniences of the day.

Wills's work was featured in *Life* magazine and the *Saturday Evening Post,* and he wrote several practical books for homebuilders and homeowners that listed

ABOVE, **Royal Barry Wills is credited** with reviving the Cape in a manner consistent with its seventeenth-century origins. To that end, this Cape is built low to the ground, with several ells that imply the house had been expanded over several generations.

LEFT, **Although Wills's smallest houses** were built with economy in mind, they were composed with great care. The front elevation, with its classic gable, or doghouse, dormers, is symmetrically arranged around the center chimney.

A Cape addition doesn't have to adhere strictly to a historical model, even when the main house hews close to the norm. A bank of windows can capitalize on a view that the home had never embraced.

plans for sale. In his 1946 book, *Planning Your Home Wisely!* (Franklin Watts, 1946), he wrote, "I suppose the reason Cape Cod Houses are so popular is that they are the simplest expression of shelter. They lend themselves to a minimum of detail and a maximum of comfort." The Wills signature Cape is still being built today, as the second and third generations continue in the family firm, Royal Barry Wills and Associates, in Boston.

THE CAPING OF AMERICA

Construction slowed to a trickle during the Great Depression of the 1930s, and resources during the early 1940s were directed to the war effort. Finally, at the end of World War II, housing construction took off again. Other enterprising developers adopted the Cape, and hundreds of Cape-filled neighborhoods sprung up in the late 1940s and 1950s, offering affordable housing for returning servicemen and their young families. More homes were built during this boom than ever before in American history. The growth was in part allowed by

ABOVE, **The old cabinets** were refinished and reconfigured when this kitchen was renovated, allowing the owners to put their dollars into good appliances, fancy light fixtures, and stone countertops.

LEFT, **A graceful pedestal** sink just inside the back door and, beyond, sleek wood floors. They're a match, and suit this Cape.

the availability of inexpensive land that had been beyond the reach of streetcar lines but was accessible by car; the nation's highway system was expanding, and cars were relatively affordable. Another factor behind the growth was that construction processes had become streamlined. At the same time, appliances and materials were again rolling out of factories that had been temporarily devoted to the war effort.

The new developments formed suburbs in concentric bands around city centers. The largest, such as Levittown in Long Island, New York, and Lakewood, near Los Angeles, were nearly the size of cities themselves (see the sidebar on p. 24).

As popular as the new suburbs were, critics called them homogenous, lowbrow, and even tacky. True, the houses in these developments were built in assembly-line fashion and often appeared virtually identical, with only mirror-image differences. Nevertheless, the first wave of owners was delighted. These "Little Boxes," as they were lampooned in a popular song of the 1960s, represented a step up economically and were certainly an improvement on the crowded city apartments that many people had known. The American Dream of owning one's own home was finally available to a great number of families

Cape neighborhoods were planned around an important new fixture in middle-class life, the family car. Before World War II, most modest homes had narrow front yards, because there was no need to park a car on the property—homeowners relied on streetcars for transportation. But in Levittown and other postwar suburbs, lots were significantly wider, at least 60 ft., to accommodate a driveway along one side. For first-time homeowners, the car was as important a symbol of the

Life in a Cape Community

WHEN WE BOUGHT OUR CAPE, it had been little improved since it was built in 1948. We were only the third owners in nearly 50 years, and the original wallpaper still graced the dining room walls. Our next-door-but-one neighbor, Harry, had been the lead carpenter on all the houses built in this neighborhood of Capes. Harry was quite hard of hearing in his later years, but as soon as anyone on the street pulled out a hammer to hang a picture, let alone do some major improvements, he was on the spot to make sure his handiwork wouldn't be harmed.

We loved our little house, but it needed a few changes. When we embarked on our kitchen overhaul, Harry approved of our design, especially since we planned on recycling "his" kitchen cabinets into a new configuration. Since that endeavor, we've completed the second phase of our multiphased master plan—a family room that takes advantage of our view of the stream running through the backyard. Harry is not here to see it, but I think that he would have approved.

Roofs can be fun rather than just a shingled slope. A variety of dormer sizes enlivens the front elevation of this Cape.

new era as the house itself. In centuries past, houses had been oriented to the sun, but now lots were laid out to accommodate the automobile. As you drive down any of countless Maple Streets across the country, there is a familiar rhythm to the driveways as they intersect the curb.

GETTING WITH THE TIMES

Depending on when your Cape was built in this long timeline, it may be more than ready for either an ambitious addition or a modest makeover that addresses the way you live today. As a sign of how things have

changed since the 1950s, consider the way in which we describe our lives. We prefer *hanging out* in the family room to *entertaining* in the living room. We casually *party* rather than *throw a party,* and we invite our guests into the kitchen to help us cook. And although we probably don't like to admit it, we don't have sit-down family dinners in the dining room every night. In some households, the norm is to pull up a stool at the kitchen counter, pop in a video, and eat take-out pizza while watching "Iron Giant" for the umpteenth time. Also, more of us than ever have sworn off commuting

Little-used porches and sunrooms are ripe for transformation into year-round living spaces.

long distances to work in favor of a computer and a home office.

We also have a lot more stuff than our parents' generation ever contended with. The appliances that we rely on every day—clothes dryer, dishwasher, answering machine, audio systems, vacuum cleaners, televisions and VCRs, and home computers—all need to find a place somewhere under that steeply pitched roof. Furniture is also bigger than before. Your overstuffed leather fold-out couch eats up a lot more space than the chintz-covered early American settee that sat in Aunt Ruby's parlor.

The privacy requirements of most families have changed, too. We want each child to have his or her own bedroom, and kids now need more space for all their toys, stereos, and computers. We expect plenty of bathrooms, and even a small house is considered "underimproved" if it has fewer than two.

And finally, no matter what the style, Cape or not, we share a greater desire for comfort in our homes. Despite the photographs of stark houses in architectural magazines, Spartan homes are not particularly livable. As author and architect Witold Rybczynski puts it in his "Onion Theory of Comfort" from *Home: A Short History of an Idea* (Viking Penguin, 1986), "Comfort is both simple and complicated. It incorporates many transparent layers of meaning—privacy, ease, convenience—some of which are buried deeper than others."

Choosing a Strategy

It's daunting to begin any building project, especially a major one that will alter your living conditions and cost a good deal. You'll want to have a master plan that reflects the daily life of the household. If you've had the chance to live in your Cape a while, you will have had a chance to observe patterns that are particular to your house and your way of doing things: how sunlight comes into the house at various seasons and times of day, what the natural path is from the car to the house, and which exterior door you use most frequently.

Be a little bold as you rethink your home. Why commit an entire room to a suite of uncomfortable and overformal furniture? Formality does not go well with a Cape Cod house. Why restrict a breakfast nook to toast and coffee, when you desperately need a place to put your computer? This is your house, and it should be furnished to suit your needs rather than according to the standards of advertisers, home magazines, and nosy neighbors.

The tub placement makes the most of the low space under the eaves. With all of that fenestration, bathers are apt to feel like they're skinny-dipping.

When a Cape visually explodes like this, it helps to retain some of its characteristics in order to keep the whole project coherent.

As you consider ways to renovate, remodel, or enlarge your Cape, I suggest you make a list of activities or a description of places (rather than room names) that you need in your house. If you limited your life's activities to the tasks suggested by the room names in a typical Cape—bathing, dining, living—you would have a very dull life. Architects call this exercise *programming,* and it is useful in organizing yourself and clarifying your expectations. For example, your list might include "a place to sew" rather than a sewing room. This could result in the design of a special counter in the kitchen or family room that houses all your sewing supplies, so that you can put your paraphernalia away neatly when you are not using it. And you might not have to take up a whole room at the expense of other activities.

THINKING SMALL

If you love the look of a Cape but have either a limited budget or tight lot, you may want to explore the ways in which a house can be expanded without pushing beyond its current footprint. An excellent (and traditional) way of improving your upstairs rooms is to add dormers to capture more headroom and light. Dormers may be as small as a single window in width, or they can encompass the length of the attic. Nothing is more characteristic of a Cape bedroom than the nooks and crannies that a dormered roof creates.

Or your home may have a porch, sunroom, or garage that just never lived up to its potential and might be incorporated into the home proper by turning it into a year-round room. And then there are remodelings that don't seize new territory, but make the home more livable by reordering what's already under the roof. With

plenty of brainstorming (and perhaps the help of an architect who has been through this many times before), you may be able to arrive at the house you're after by moving walls, switching the roles of rooms, and/or making new windows. Chapter 2 looks at how other homeowners have worked major changes with modest means.

ADDING ON

Most people, when they envision an addition, see the house growing something—a wing or at least a protrusion of some kind. Chapter 3 suggests how to enlarge and update a home without losing that Cape look. Historically, Capes underwent many transformations and gained additions while still retaining their Cape-ness. Take a look at historical models like the one shown below. Depending on the spaces that you want, there are several tried-and-true design directions that will work to maintain your home's Cape flavor.

As for the size of additions, they look best if they don't overwhelm the original Cape structure. By maintaining the hierarchy of forms—that is, keeping the pieces distinct, rather than equal in size—you will go a long way to keeping your Cape true to its historic ori-

gins. The objective is to build a collection of smaller pieces, rather than erecting an envelope that blurs the original Cape's form.

Making changes in gradual steps also allows you to stay within your budget, while making the inconveniences during construction less painful. One of the difficulties in enlarging a Cape is that you can't get away from it all by moving into a distant wing. Its few rooms and limited dimensions preclude blocking off a portion to live in while the work is being done on another portion of the house.

NEW OR RADICALLY RENEWED

You can really give tradition a good stretch if that's what suits your needs. After all, the colonists themselves saw no need to freeze their own houses in time. So, changing the style—even if it means greatly altering the Cape form—might be the approach for you. As one house in Chapter 3 suggests, it might be best to eliminate the Cape look all together by turning your house into a full two-story home.

Finally, you might want to bypass the whole process of undoing an older home's legacy and build a new Cape, as Americans have been doing for more than 300 years. Chapter 4 offers ideas that will help get you started on designing a home from the ground up, either with traditional details or in an eclectic manner.

The projects in the following chapters are meant to inspire, not to show the way. There is no such thing as a textbook renovation, a completely accurate remodel, or an exact reproduction, because the variables are so many. Even though you will be living in a home with a grand heritage that spans the centuries and the Atlantic, it's good to keep in mind that a classic style survives because of a characteristic elasticity. Its hallmarks are highly malleable and not easily dented, so proceed boldly.

The Timothy Wood House, Halifax, Massachusetts.

For a home that looks homey rather than high-falutin', look for ways of breaking up the structure's mass into a series of smaller elements.

CHAPTER TWO

MODEST REMODELS

ABOVE, **The need for display shelves** inspired this comfy feature that is part window seat and part bookcase.

FACING PAGE, **Unlike the decoy-encrusted country** kitchens of a few years back, this room does not shout out the fact that it is in a historic Cape. The recently installed cabinets don't look like vintage units, but in their detailing they recall traditional furniture.

W ITH ITS TYPICALLY MODEST DIMENSIONS, a Cape can feel either cozy or confining. And that in turn depends not only on how many people you have under the roof but also on how well the floor plan is working.

There may be no place to greet guests when they arrive, so that you have to shoo them straight into the living room (Cape entries tend to be cramped or nonexistent). It could be that the dining room isn't long enough to make use of the table's second leaf (chances are the dining room is "formal" but not necessarily gracious). A circa-1952 kitchen may be too small for two cooks and a desperately needed dishwasher. Upstairs, your child's bedroom may not have enough space to allow for a good, rousing pillow fight, much less sleepovers. And, in a Cape, family members might know the unsettling experience of sitting upright in bed and bumping their heads against that characteristically sloped ceiling.

Circumstances like these start many of us Cape owners daydreaming about a renovation or small addition—changes just ambitious enough to set things right. The goal isn't a drop-dead palace in tasteful gray shingles, but a home that works well in an unassuming way. Of course, even small jobs have to be budgeted. And the slightest rearrangements of the floor plan will generate an unbelievable amount of dust, debris, and disruption. We tend to forget that improvements typically involve the process of *unbuilding.* This may mean correcting a disjointed layout, punching a hole in a wall for a window, or tearing away shingles to cap the Cape with a couple of dormers.

Big Plans for a Small Area

You may be able to create a remarkable amount of useful space without adding an inch to the footprint of your Cape. Two popular projects are grafting on a bay window and adding a dormer to create a sunny bedroom. And an addition can be a subtle (and relatively inexpensive) matter of bumping out just one wall several feet to transform the room within. Even something as minor as a new porch or simple roof overhang will welcome visitors, allow you to stand out of the rain while fumbling for your keys, and protect a handcrafted wood door from the elements.

This chapter looks at relatively small-scale ways in which Capes have overcome their limitations. Any of these projects can be seen through without throwing the baby out with the bath water. Because they are focused rather than sweeping, the best aspects of your Cape will likely remain intact. Here is your opportunity to personalize one special room, to feature a treasured collection, to display an heirloom corner cupboard, or to set aside a quiet retreat for music or reflection. Every

ABOVE, **Traditionally styled Capes** never had the luxury of a covered front stoop. This minor addition adds a wealth of comfort on a rainy day when visitors call. Simple detailing at the railings and post tie this small front porch into the Cape aesthetic.

FACING PAGE, **A second-floor sitting room** certainly isn't the first living space a family would put on its must-have list, but this is a pleasant spot for a late-night brandy or an early-morning coffee.

individual, every family has particular patterns for living that can be better supported by a rearrangement of walls, doors, and windows.

Modernizing at the Core

For reasons best known to each of us, remodeling kitchens and baths is the most common renovation job. If your Cape has been unaltered since it was built, then there's no mystery—these rooms are likely crying out for new fixtures and materials. Even if the Cape's kitchen and bath have already been modernized, these rooms are quick to show their age, in terms of both wear and tear and changing fashion. This could be your incentive for gutting the room and starting over, perhaps opening up the kitchen to an adjacent room

or even moving it off to a more convenient area of the house.

THE KITCHEN AS FAMILY ROOM

The kitchens of postwar Capes are notoriously small, and if the home is largely unimproved chances are this room is an isolated place where meal preparation and the drudgery of cleanup take place behind closed doors. In the 1950s, you may recall, dinner materialized magically from the kitchen and was placed before the family by Mother in her pumps and pearls.

Today, few families choose to segregate food preparation to such a degree, and there has been an easing of the barrier between family room, dining area, and kitchen. The resulting space has become the nucleus of the

Shoehorning a powder room under a stairway in an old Cape requires a bit of ingenuity and a willingness to give up storage in favor of convenience.

home—the true family room—where we socialize, work on crafts, do homework, and watch movies. If square footage is at a premium, you can create a generous-size dine-in kitchen, in which a single table is used for all meals, for both adults and young people. (After all, it's always more fun at the kids' table!)

A BETTER BATHROOM

The very first Cape owners made do with outhouses and washtubs, so there is no historic model for a colonial Cape bathroom (unless you want to feature a crescent-shaped outhouse window in your design). In Capes built just after World War II, a single bathroom was the norm. It would be on the first floor, probably between the two bedrooms. And it was a workhorse,

Kitchen Overhaul

THIS NORTHWESTERN CAPE'S old kitchen was dim and cramped, and it suffered from "minimal counter space and excess circulation," in the words of architect George Ostrow. A total redesign was in order, one that would acknowledge the owners' entertaining style and incorporate the work of local craftspeople.

The existing kitchen had no dishwasher, and the door was the only access to the deck out back.

The alder veneer kitchen cabinets and cast concrete island countertop were selected in lieu of more conventional materials. The bench and table were locally made out of cherry and alder.

ABOVE, **Are you relaxed enough** to enjoy mingling with guests while preparing a meal? If so, give some thought to having the kitchen visible from the living room, rather then shutting off the food preparation area. In this home, guests can circulate into the graciously appointed kitchen without feeling that they have stumbled into the sequestered family end of the house.

LEFT, **Capes often have** something that opulent new homes don't—a window in the bathroom. The pattern on the floor—small black diamonds between larger tiles of white—is an old standard that connotes cleanliness.

Some homeowners like sequestered, private spaces, and others prefer their interior walls few and far between. The living and family rooms of this house seem more spacious now that walls have been removed, and the new arrangement makes the most of views to the backyard.

meeting the needs of everyone under the roof—sequentially, of course, not simultaneously, because it wasn't that large. Since then, Americans have come to expect at least two bathrooms in all but the most modest dwellings.

That single ground-floor bathroom may be sufficient if only one or two people live in your home (even though all your grooming products and beauty secrets will be on view when company calls). But doing without a second bath becomes a challenge in a larger household, when kids in bathrobes clamor for their turn. And then there are the limb-threatening trips downstairs to the bathroom at night. If you add a bath to your Cape, the efficient location is upstairs, directly above the original one so that the new plumbing runs are straightforward.

Working with What You've Got

Before committing yourself to a new addition to solve your domestic woes, stop to examine how well your current rooms are working. You may find that you spend 80 percent of your time in just 20 percent of the house. If so, it could be a better idea to reconfigure those rooms or improve the connections between them.

Removing a few interior walls, polishing up the kitchen, and adding a bank of French doors can make a house seem much bigger inside. This doesn't mean simply creating one large room; instead, it's ideal to maintain separate and distinct spaces. The result will be a house that seems bigger and more richly layered, having many particular places within it. Note that by creating long diagonal views through the house, you are able to see more than one space at a time, further stretching the plan's apparent size.

A built-in hutch flanks the breakfast table in this beach-front house on Cape Cod. Beadboard paneling is used at the back of the glass-fronted cabinet and continues down to the counter and up to the similarly faced ceiling.

Pushing Out to the Street

BECAUSE THIS HOME'S gable end faced the street, architect Jeffrey Rubin was able to add onto its front side. He extruded an addition along the existing roof pitch, creating a welcoming front porch at the same time.

Confined entry impeded flow.

Before

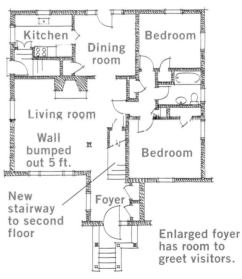

After

This Cape grew by acquiring an entry porch and pushing out the front wall of the living room. In the process, the facade gained two smaller gable ends, making the home's appearance more engaging.

Architect Mark Halstead called this a "Cape reclamation." Leaving the basic box of the addition intact, he added roof overhangs on all sides to make the two-story structure look like a one-story wing with a pair of shed dormers. It's an illusion, and one that works very well—the suggestion of a reduced scale is in keeping with the original Cape (shown below).

Modest Isn't Mundane

Just because a potential project is small doesn't mean it can't be interesting and even highly dramatic. A minor architectural flaw often stimulates a solution that adds more than just headroom or a few square feet. For example, the need for a simple roof overhang at the front steps might grow into a roomy front porch with a spot for a bench. You could bring more daylight into a dreary corner with a simple window, but why not consider a deep bay and comfy window seat? An ordinary kitchen or bathroom renovation can become much more if you take the time to consider elegant yet simple details, artfully crafted. This added level of attention can cost more, of course, but renovating on a modest scale may allow you to spend more on trim, or

Many Cape owners particularly like the alcoves formed by the sloping ceiling planes of the second floor.

A Dormer Dictionary

DORMERS COME in several shapes and many sizes and range from easily overlooked add-ons to somewhat outrageous features that change the entire personality of a house.

A shed dormer simply has a flat roof with a relatively shallow pitch, allowing one or more windows to be inserted between its two side walls. A gable dormer has a gable roof, its ridge running perpendicular to that of the house; it is sometimes known as a doghouse dormer because of its characteristic shape. A Nantucket dormer is more complex, taking the form of two gable dormers connected by a shed dormer. Dormers also can have hipped or even curved roofs.

While some dormers are just big enough to admit a little daylight and fresh air, shed dormers can stretch nearly the entire width of a Cape, greatly increasing the usable square footage of the second floor.

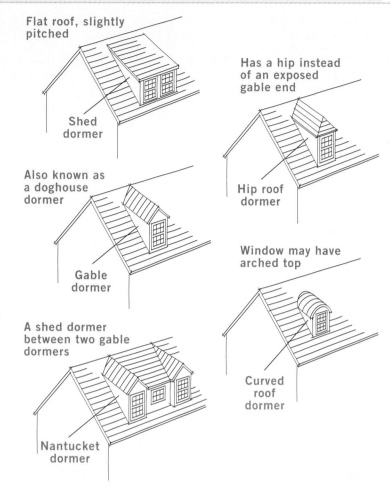

Flat roof, slightly pitched

Shed dormer

Has a hip instead of an exposed gable end

Hip roof dormer

Also known as a doghouse dormer

Gable dormer

Window may have arched top

A shed dormer between two gable dormers

Curved roof dormer

Nantucket dormer

---

a finer grade of materials, or more built-ins, or the services of an architect whose work you've admired in other homes. A small project, if well conceived and carried out, can do more to embellish a Cape than a grand addition that's short on character.

Underfoot and Overhead

Another way of working with what you've got is to carve out new rooms from spaces that may be right under your nose (in the basement) or overhead (in an unfinished part of the attic). You might even convert an under-used porch into a year-round room. By making

better use of the area you already have under your roof, you'll almost certainly spend less than for a major expansion. And, you won't end up with vestigial spaces that are barely visited, like a formal living room that is ignored in favor of a new, cheery family room with kitchen.

The unfinished space up under a Cape's rafters can be called an attic, but this undersells the potential of the area. If your Cape has a stairway leading up to this level, you are already on your way to creating a beautiful suite of rooms. Most likely, the top step lands somewhere in the middle of the second floor, yielding two potential rooms, one at each end of the house. With just a window or two in the gable walls, these rooms are probably dim, and the headroom is limited. But that gloom can be banished relatively inexpensively by putting in a couple of dormers and perhaps a skylight. And dormers increase the useable floor space by raising the headroom. For the price, this is the most dramatic transformation that can happen to Cape.

Back porches are not customarily thought of as part of a Cape's standard equipment, but they are often eventually added—some more successfully than others. If you have a porch that is seldom used, think about converting it to a family room, sunroom, or den. Given that the porch starts you off with a roof and some sort of foundation, it may not cost a great deal to fill in the open sides with windows and insulated walls, update and insulate the floors and ceiling, and add heat and electricity.

ABOVE, **Dormers create** interesting spaces where they intersect with the pitch of a roof. Here, a triangular opportunity is used for a built-in desk and shelving.

BELOW, **Unfinished basements** are an option for additional living space. Here, an open stairway wraps around a fireplace and leads down to a bright playroom.

When Dowdy Won't Do

ABOVE, **The roof overhang** with supporting brackets was added to both protect the back door and punctuate the bland rear elevation of this house.

FACING PAGE, **The storage wall** between kitchen and dining room combines a display area above with cabinets below.

K AT, A LANDSCAPE ARCHITECT, AND KEVIN, AN architect, collaborated on the renovation of this 1920s Cape in suburban Connecticut. The house had two downstairs bedrooms that would become his and hers offices, a combination of kitchen, living room, and dining room that suited entertaining, and an upstairs master suite. But like many older homes, the place needed to be spruced up both outside and in, and a coat of paint and new furniture would simply not do the trick.

Years of neglect had taken their toll on the outside of this house, and the place looked dowdy and well worn. New six-over-one cottage-style windows and authentic wood shutters were installed throughout to unify the facade, replacing a mongrel collection of mismatched window types. The exterior was resurfaced with cedar siding and asphalt roof shingles, with rebuilt eaves to encase rotted rafter tails. The back door onto the deck was fitted with a roof supported by lyrical brackets. In the front, the existing portico sheltering the door retains its arched ceiling, but it was trimmed with a new gable pediment.

A **new front** portico and matching windows revived this Cape's facade. Six-over-one cottage-style windows impart a storybook air.

OPENING UP THE INTERIOR

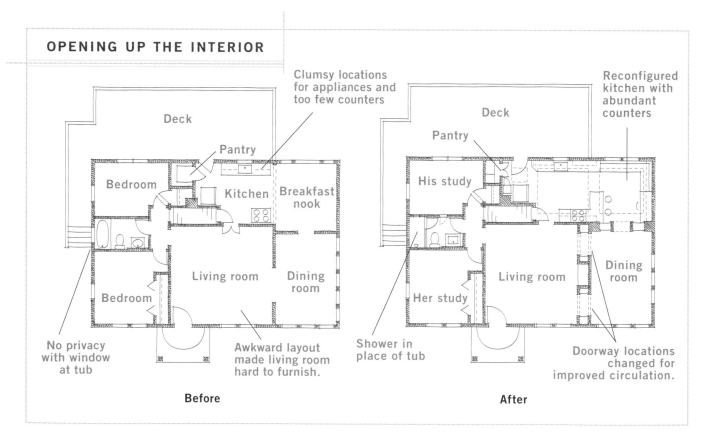

Clumsy locations for appliances and too few counters

Deck

Pantry

Bedroom

Kitchen

Breakfast nook

Living room

Dining room

Bedroom

No privacy with window at tub

Awkward layout made living room hard to furnish.

Before

Reconfigured kitchen with abundant counters

Deck

Pantry

His study

Living room

Dining room

Her study

Shower in place of tub

Doorway locations changed for improved circulation.

After

Portals and Built-Ins

Inside, the couple was willing to sacrifice walls to trade the home's sequestered rooms for the fresh open spaces you see here. In a conventional layout, the rooms are an aggregation of boxes, each with one or two doorways to an adjoining box. It all makes perfect sense when you look at a floor plan, but this segregated approach never quite allows you to get an impression of the home's full size.

Kat and Kevin's new layout allows each room to borrow vistas and daylight from other areas, for an architectural version of symbiosis. The use of bright colors—white trim throughout and white or gold for the walls—makes the most of this effect. Except for the kitchen, the original floors are old-growth **quarter-sawn** heartwood pine, refinished to show off their rich color.

ABOVE, **Sticking doorways** symmetrically into walls is a no-brainer for the builder but may not be the best arrangement for the home's layout.

BELOW, **Two new doorways** into the dining room redirect the circulation to the perimeter of the living room, for a traffic flow that won't interrupt conversation—or TV watching.

quarter-sawn Wood sawn from the log to emphasize the grain, often used with oak.

Spicing Up the Kitchen

IN THE 1950S, when many thousands of Capes were built, the goal was streamlined modernity. The kitchen was treated to new plastic laminates and vinyl tiles, and the floor plans strictly adhered to the work triangle, specifying certain optimal distances from stove to refrigerator to sink. Appliance manufacturers came up with standardized counter heights and depths to accommodate their products.

These design standards were developed in the name of efficiency, but they ignore the kitchen's orientation to other rooms, the quality of sunlight or a view, and the needs particular to each homeowner.

For your Cape, this might mean adding a window to catch a view of the approaching school bus, putting in a pass-through to the dining room, or simply installing hooks for a treasured collection of copper pans. Don't feel restrained by a formula of ideal dimensions. A person of small stature or a serious baker might prefer counters at a lower height. And while a big kitchen makes sense for a family that loves to prepare meals from scratch, it might be an expensive luxury for those who do their cooking in a microwave. As for materials, easy-to-clean practicality doesn't have to mean using only plastic laminates. A variety of materials and colors will enliven the kitchen and make it seem more of a living space than a work room.

Two doorways replaced the single opening between the living and dining rooms. These portals incorporate a thick storage wall that contains the television, stereo, and home library rather than dominating the wall spaces in the adjacent rooms. These units are well lit, and when other lights are low, the portals form a curtain of illumination between the rooms.

Most renovations increase the number of windows, but two were removed from the dining room to allow enough wall space for displaying art. The wall between the dining room and the kitchen also has a thick dimension, and the doorway through it is flanked by glass display shelves for decorative barware, visible from both sides.

A Kitchen Conversion

The old kitchen had plenty of area but not much of it was devoted to counters and storage. The refrigerator huddled in its corner like a hesitant waiter, and the stove was marooned apart from the counters. There was a good-size breakfast nook, but it seemed redundant because the dining room table was just a few steps away. So the owners decided to put the space to better use.

To save money for relatively expensive touches, the locations of the sink, stove, and refrigerator weren't changed. Kat and Kevin splurged instead on polished Italian granite countertops and custom cabinetry. The new stove sits within a bank of counters, with a granite-topped peninsula to one side that now serves the function of the former breakfast nook. The nook has been reborn as the home's planning center, with a phone and built-in desk. This is the perfect spot to toss down car keys, arrange a social calendar, and pay household bills. There's a bench with storage cabinets below, suited to sipping coffee or hanging out with a drink before dinner.

There were no radical physical changes in this remodeling. The house's overall dimensions didn't change. The alterations are "experiential," as Kevin puts it, in that they yield an improved quality of space instead of more square feet.

ABOVE, **A built-in bench** in the kitchen is a space-conserving approach to adding informal seating.

LEFT, **Capes don't often** come with command centers, and you may want to study your home for a spot that is both close at hand and also spared the buffeting of passing foot traffic.

Room at the Top

ABOVE, **A new addition** peeks over the ridge and invites daylight into the window-less interior space below.

FACING PAGE, **Although a major renovation** involves lots of big decisions, the little ones count as well. Take the time to make the most of the home's nooks and crannies. Here, an upstairs hallway has a mini-library tucked alongside the stairway.

H AVING A HOME OFFICE AT ONE END OF THE master bedroom seemed like a good idea at the time. But for Jane and Wayne, the fax machine sounding off at night was the catalyst for a renovation. Their brick Cape, located in a tidy Minnesota neighborhood, had all the right elements, but the elements were all on the same floor so that the couple felt as if they were living in an apartment. They looked to the unfinished attic for a solution.

As in many Capes, the stairs were in place, there were windows (a few) up there, and the area was waiting to be exploited. For architect Robert Gerloff, this was an inviting scenario—he would have nothing to undo before tackling that raw space.

Up under the Roof

In their discussions with Robert, Jane and Wayne outlined what they expected out of the attic—a master bedroom, a bedroom for their son, a bathroom, and a sitting room. This would allow two downstairs bedrooms to become a full-time home office and a den. To make the most of the square footage under the roof, Robert added a large gable dormer that is cantilevered

Arch-top windows have become an architectural cliché, and they often don't fit the homes they embellish. But if carefully considered as part of the overall design, they can add interest to a facade.

out over the back wall of the house. He accomplished this structurally by sistering, or bolting, new floor joists to the existing ones over the kitchen.

This dormer is occupied by the master bedroom, with a ceiling that follows the pitch of the gable roof. Doubled **collar ties** boldly spring from the sloping planes. Head height was maximized by a trick that's easy to overlook from the ground below. The new gable dormer rises higher than the house itself, and the overlap creates a triangular window above the central ridge. Daylight from this window spills into the center of the second floor, where it is most needed.

The remaining space on the second floor is divided between the son's bedroom and the gallery, so-called

Sky Windows

CAPE DETAILS ☆

EVEN WITH DORMERS the second floor of a Cape can be somewhat short on daylight. Skylights are an alternate way of bringing natural light into these rooms while maintaining the roofline, an important consideration if you want to keep the straightforward, uncluttered look of a traditional Cape. Operable models provide a measure of ventilation as well. Some have integral blinds to shield late sleepers from the sun's rays.

Skylights generally come in widths that conform to standard rafter spacing, in multiples of 16 in. Although they are simpler to add than dormers, some extra framing is required,

and care must be taken to flash them properly so that they are weathertight. Even though skylights aren't as visible as dormers, it's best to position them with some consideration of the home's facade so that they don't appear to be an afterthought. If they can be seen easily from the yard or the street, try to align them with the windows below.

The collar ties were beefed up with thicker framing to provide a decorative element under the sloping roof of this master bedroom, making a design asset out of a structural necessity.

collar tie — A horizontal framing member that spans a pair of rafters to help keep the roof true.

because it does more than conduct traffic in the manner of a hall. At 5 ft. wide, the gallery is wide enough for pieces of furniture and to allow children to stretch out and play. It is flanked by a sturdy bookcase that runs the length of the stair.

It is interesting that these homeowners were content with only one bathroom upstairs. Rather than devote floor space to a master bath, they opted for a single spacious family bathroom. The tub has been placed at the low side of the room, which makes good sense—if you bathe sitting down, that is, because it wasn't possible to install a shower head. The room has a separate shower stall to get around that limitation. By the tub, inset shelves display part of Jane's pottery collection. To give the second floor a cottage-like atmosphere, beadboard was used for the walls in the bathroom as well as the shelves in the gallery.

ABOVE, **Display a collection** in the bathroom? Sure, as long as the collectibles are relatively waterproof.

RIGHT, **A wraparound wall** and bookcase conceal the stairway to the first floor and define a play space for the kids.

INTO THE ATTIC

Cramped for too long on the first floor, the homeowners expanded into the unfinished attic. The ridge of the new master bedroom stands just above that of the house itself, for higher ceilings.

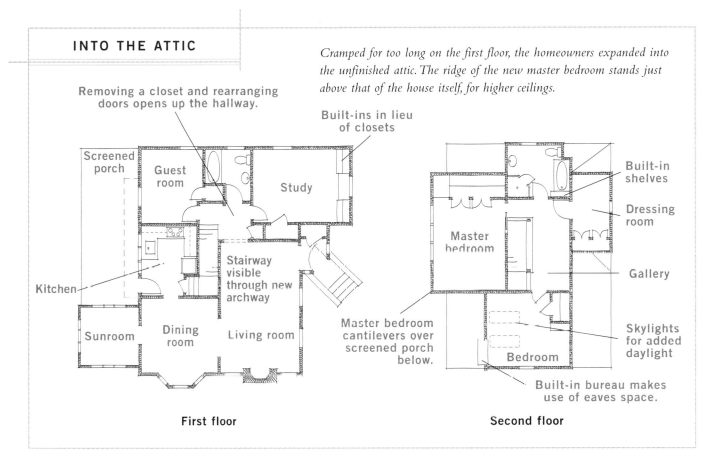

Removing a closet and rearranging doors opens up the hallway.

Built-ins in lieu of closets

Screened porch

Guest room

Study

Kitchen

Stairway visible through new archway

Sunroom

Dining room

Living room

First floor

Built-in shelves

Dressing room

Master bedroom

Gallery

Master bedroom cantilevers over screened porch below.

Skylights for added daylight

Bedroom

Built-in bureau makes use of eaves space.

Second floor

One way to squeeze all the storage you can out of a moderate-size Cape is to set drawers into the kneewalls of bedrooms. Ready-made units are marketed for just this application.

57

A Stairway Upgrade

☆ **THE STAIRWAYS** of postwar Capes were rarely anything special, because they typically didn't lead to anyplace special. If you turn the second floor into handsome living quarters, you may want to improve or replace the stairs to keep up to the standard of their new destination.

The simplest approach is to leave the existing treads and risers and install a new balustrade and newel post with architectural interest. To make the stairway a more visible feature, you can remove all or part of the walls enclosing it; at the same time, this will have the effect of adding to the apparent square footage of the first floor.

If you are putting in a new stairway, you can save money by specifying softwood construction and then painting the stairs, for a look consistent with early homes. The longest-wearing construction is of hardwood—oak or ash—for years of low-maintenance service.

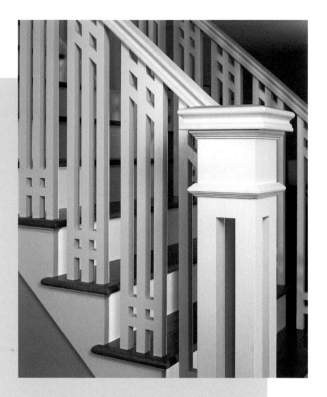

The custom-crafted newel and balustrade that dress up this stairway were assembled from stock parts available at any lumberyard.

A Glass Act

Robert pulled out all the stops in distributing sunlight throughout the second floor. The window at the back of the new gable dormer directs some light into the master bedroom via an interior window. French doors filter additional light into the gallery from the dressing room that sits at the front of the house in an existing shed dormer. The child's bedroom is tucked under the roof and has only one standard window, but a pair of skylights were added for light and air circulation, without the expense or possible visual clutter of tacking on a third dormer.

This is another Cape that humbly displays its architectural flourishes only when you step inside or circle around to the privacy of the backyard. The most notable feature, the master bedroom's impressive window array, is played down—both windows and trim are painted the same color as the walls, as elsewhere in the house, for a subtle effect that seems to befit a Cape. Even the screens of the back porch are toned to blend in with the rest of the facade.

By building in bookcases around a window, you can frame a window seat. The seat can offer storage or mask a bulky radiator.

Instant Tradition

An uninspired Cape with an overgrown backyard seemed an unlikely choice for Robert Norris, an architect and enthusiastic gardener. He was drawn to the Georgia climate, which would allow gracious living (and gardening) throughout the seasons. But the Cape's layout was little more than a collection of self-contained compartments that failed to take advantage of the pleasant weather, except for the solarium off the dining room.

Robert wanted his Cape to resemble an old-world country cottage, and he set about building in a historic patina while making the house more livable as well. There would have to be bright and welcoming spaces as well as views to the garden that, at first, grew only in his imagination.

Built-In History

Robert began by reconfiguring the first floor to overcome a couple of limitations, one of which was obvious as soon as you walked in the front door. Visitors stepped inside to be greeted by the view of a shocking pink bathroom—a floor-plan flaw not uncommon in small Capes, if there isn't a more private place to place the facilities. Also, the living room and family room were divided by the stairway in an awkward fashion.

This cottage was once a 1970s standard builder's Cape. The owner wanted a relaxed, romantic look and used a number of details to work the change. The mix of materials on the front elevation adds layers of texture that invite a second look.

balustrade—A row of balusters, or vertical spindles, beneath a hand rail.

colonnade—A row of columns supporting a horizontal element of some kind.

By shifting walls and enlarging doorways, Robert blocked the view of the bathroom and created a clear line of sight from the entry through the living room to the sunny family room. The doorways were trimmed with generous casings to emphasize these portals in a way that encourages guests to circulate through the house. Visual cues of this sort can help direct both the eye and the flow of traffic, making a compromised floor plan work much better.

One wall along the stair was replaced with an unusual **balustrade**—decidedly not a New England balustrade. Its geometric design is adapted from classic Southern Chippendale–inspired motifs found at Monticello and other houses of that era.

The original family room was cramped and unembellished save for a pair of 1970s-era patio sliders out to the deck. Robert revitalized this unlovable space by opening up the room at one end to the decorative stairway and then bumping it out 5 ft. into the yard in the other direction. A wide bank of French doors frames the view to the back garden. The doors are extra tall and made to order, with oversize muntins in an unusual horizontal arrangement that allows for larger panes of glass. This pattern is another clear break with New England tradition, which is characterized by small, delicately delineated panes. A **colonnade** beyond the room supports a bold second-floor **cross-gable**.

A Faux Old House

The family room extension connects directly to a breakfast room addition, a new feature that's intended to look as though it had evolved through the years.

Even if your Cape lacks a foyer and the front door delivers guests unceremoniously into the living room, long views through the rooms will help make the home more inviting.

cross-gable — A portion of gable roof projecting at right angles from the main roof.

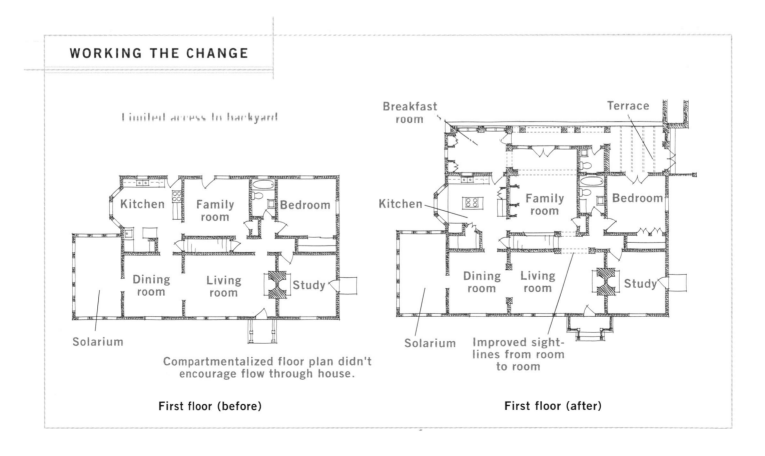

WORKING THE CHANGE

Limited access to backyard

Kitchen | Family room | Bedroom

Dining room | Living room | Study

Solarium

Compartmentalized floor plan didn't encourage flow through house.

First floor (before)

Breakfast room | Terrace

Kitchen | Family room | Bedroom

Dining room | Living room | Study

Solarium | Improved sight-lines from room to room

First floor (after)

FACING PAGE, **Flagstone isn't just** for the garden. The architect deliberately detailed this breakfast room to imply that it was once was a porch.

RIGHT, **The beadboard ceiling** is new to this 1960s Cape, but it suggests that the house might be from an earlier era. The oval window over the sink gives a view into the breakfast room.

Robert used a stone floor, **board-and-batten** walls, and exposed hewn beams so that you might think this was once a covered porch that had been enclosed to make a pleasant room. That's one way of adding a measure of history to a home—implying that there has been a series of changes over the years. (A related strategy for the *outside* of the home is to break up a large new addition into several parts to suggest that the assemblage had evolved gradually.)

The kitchen shares this vintage look. Robert added the beadboard ceiling and retrimmed the existing kitchen cabinets with rope molding for a furniture-like flourish. The cabinets were whitewashed in an uneven way so that the finish looks as if it might have been worn by years of use. An oval window was placed above the sink, where it looks into the breakfast room—it's always good to give the dish washer a view, even if only

of another room. New matching cabinets were installed within the existing bay window; the knee hole is the preferred dining spot for Robert's dog.

The second floor went through a greater transformation. Previously, the Cape had only two dreary bedrooms, with no views to the backyard. In a dramatic maneuver, the entire back slope of the roof was torn off, and then a shorter and shallower pitch was added to create a two-story-high back wall. The result is something like a Saltbox, but in reverse. The long roof slope is the newer portion on a true Saltbox, but it's the

board-and-batten — A traditional type of vertical wood siding, with narrow battens covering the spaces between wide boards.

The master bedroom ceilings were raised as high as the framing would permit and then embellished with nonstructural beams to give the sense of being in a historic house.

original pitch on this house. As a result, the home still looks quite unassuming in scale as you approach it from the front. Once in the backyard, you are you struck by just how ambitious the renovation has been.

The revived second-floor plan now includes a lavish master suite and a second guest bedroom and bath. One of the original front-facing dormers has been enlarged, giving Robert a desk alcove off the upper stair hallway.

An Uplift and a Facelift

Outside as well as in, Robert worked to ease away this Cape's signature suburban details. The use of board-and-batten siding on the dormers is an alternate treatment to clapboards or shingles and one not typically found on Capes. The new tall, slender windows suggest a time and place other than colonial New England; they are

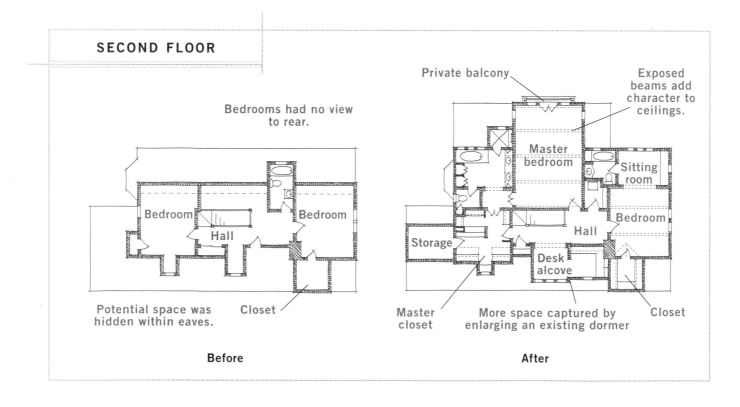

SECOND FLOOR

Bedrooms had no view to rear.

Bedroom

Bedroom

Hall

Potential space was hidden within eaves.

Closet

Before

Private balcony

Exposed beams add character to ceilings.

Master bedroom

Sitting room

Bedroom

Storage

Hall

Desk alcove

Master closet

More space captured by enlarging an existing dormer

Closet

After

ABOVE, **As elsewhere** in the house, the master bathroom has been given vintage touches such as beadboard for the walls and tub surround and the cross-buck doors on the cabinets. The shower is tucked in its own gable extension.

RIGHT, **A stone foundation wall** provides a warm backdrop for the low flowering plants. The brimming window box adds depth to the front of the house and does its part to integrate the home with its landscape.

Egress: Doors and Windows

P.T. BARNUM ONCE posted a sign inside a circus tent that said "This Way to the Egress" and charged gullible patrons a quarter to walk out and discover they'd just left the show. Egress is nothing but a fancy legal term for an exit. Building codes require you to provide a minimum number of means of egress, measuring at least a certain size, so that occupants can get out (and fire fighters get in) during an emergency.

Typical codes require that one exterior door must be of a minimum size—3 ft. wide and 6 ft. 8 in. tall is an example. The front door of most Capes will meet these criteria easily.

Minimum requirements also apply to windows in bedrooms. In many states, one window in each bedroom must be operable without the use of keys or special tools and must provide an opening of at least 5.7 sq. ft., with a minimum height of 24 in. and a minimum width of 20 in.

Codes differ from one community to the next, so when planning new construction, check with your local building officials.

ganged (or grouped) casements instead of the evenly spaced double-hungs you would expect to see on a Cape. The prominent window unit in front has a window box brimming with flowers. Its supporting brackets are hefty and handsome and add weight to what is often a visually undersized feature. Around back, the master bedroom extension has a balcony with an intricate rail that calls to mind the stairway balustrade, and this part of the house is topped off by a white **pediment,** a quotation from classic architectural heritage.

To blur the boundary between garden and home, the back elevation was made almost transparent—there is more glass than opaque wall. A parade of columns across the rear elevation implies another layer of see-through wall, and the columns enclose outdoor spaces in such a way that they feel like rooms, with lighting and furniture. An arbor suggests a ceiling overhead.

This balance of emphasis between the house and its garden reinforces the impression of the house as an English cottage. The home certainly no longer looks like a cookie-cutter Cape. The one strike against the Cape style, in some people's minds, is its relatively straightforward and unromantic personality. But as several houses in this book make clear, those basic good lines lend themselves to interpretation.

pediment — The triangular space within the gable of a roof.

Southern Comfort

ABOVE, **For an indication** of how well windows have been composed within a facade, look at the house at dusk, when the walls melt away and the glazing is lit up from within.

FACING PAGE, **A bank of casement windows** floods this kitchen with light by day. Plenty of recessed can fixtures take over after sundown.

O NE OF THE PLEASURES IN A RENOVATION project can be undoing someone else's misguided improvements. So it was with this 1949 Atlanta Cape. The 1970s had not been good to it. A lackluster floor plan and dopey detailing made Ken and Alec itch to redo the tired rooms and take advantage of missed opportunities. Their changes may seem minor on the floor plan, but the photographs tell the real story. The owners, both landscape architects, were determined to transform the house outside and in.

A Gracious Welcome

The couple worked with architect Robert Norris, owner of the house we just explored. The first change someone might notice is the gracious entryway, giving a warm Southern welcome. It is approached by a gently meandering path, rather than the original straight-shot walkway, for a "tucked-in feeling" as Alec puts it. Instead of the old porch's squared-off opening, there is now a curved portal that seems to embrace the visitor. The steps were widened and embellished with stone. The custom-made front door appears to be a pair of doors in typical Southern fashion, but it is in fact a single unit.

The window above the living room is a false dormer (top photo), added to balance the front elevation. To camouflage this bit of conceit, it is illuminated at night by a concealed light fixture.

The Tennessee fieldstone of the walkway and steps is picked up on the front facade and then continues on to form the outer wall of a "secret garden," a tiny enclosed courtyard reached from the den's French doors. In contrast to the public front lawn and the sociable rear terrace and pool, this concealed spot is ideal for a private moment or quiet breakfast.

A new trellis was installed to encourage a wisteria vine to embellish the flat rear facade of the house. A new gate and fence help define the backyard without putting up an unneighborly barrier.

The home had cheap-looking windows that gave it a blank stare, and the owners chose wood casements with traditional muntins and heavier trim. The new dormer above the living room windows also offers more than just daylight; it serves as a design device that adds a counterpoint to the window in the second-floor gable, visually balancing the facade. The architect's signature dovecote, a traditional built-in birdhouse for roost-

RIGHT, **Not all outdoor spaces** need to serve a crowd. This secret garden for two is hidden from the street by the tall stone wall.

BELOW, **Decorative gates** and fancy fences can go a long way in dressing up the border of your property.

ing doves, was placed at the top of the dining room's gable to add another cottage-like detail to the home.

A New Vision

Indoors, Ken and Alec recognized that the kitchen needed immediate attention. The shabbily constructed cabinets were installed back when leisure suits were in vogue, and they looked just as synthetic. The room simply was too small to accommodate two cooks and a couple of friends. Although there was a place to pull up

a stool, this uncomfortable spot was located at a peninsula with overhanging cabinets, right in front of the dining room door.

The solution to this kitchen's flaws was a small addition, putting the new square footage out front—the stairway prevented the kitchen from pushing into the house. Additions to Capes usually are to the rear, side, or above; but in this case it made sense to take advantage of the generously deep front yard.

The new front wall of the kitchen is stepped back slightly from the dining room, creating a slight shadow

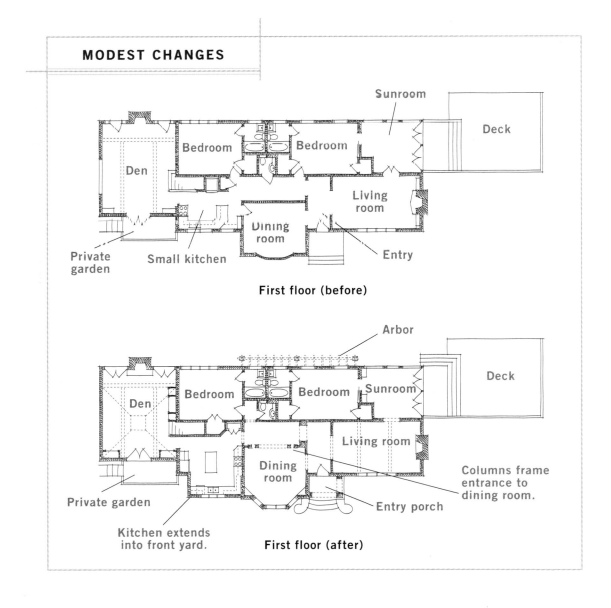

MODEST CHANGES

The enclosing wall of this dining room was opened to the adjoining hallway. The more visible the dining room, the more likely that it will be used for puzzles, games, and craft projects as well as for sharing a meal.

Sunroom

Deck

Bedroom   Bedroom

Den

Living room

Private garden   Small kitchen   Dining room   Entry

First floor (before)

Arbor

Deck

Bedroom   Bedroom   Sunroom

Den

Living room

Private garden

Dining room

Columns frame entrance to dining room.

Kitchen extends into front yard.   Entry porch

First floor (after)

The style of this balustrade looks original to the 1940s house and entirely appropriate to a Cape, and it replaces the brass and rope concoction of a previous owner.

line that outlines and emphasizes the gable at the front of the house. A good rule of thumb is never to change materials in the same plane. To do so can lead to what I call *contact paperitis,* a design flaw in which a two-dimensional flatness isn't helped by the ignoble use of contrasting materials. Here, the kitchen is faced in stone while the dining room is done in wood shingles. Beyond them, the living room and sunroom are faced in the original brick.

The kitchen's double sinks are under a new triple-sash casement. Casement or awning windows are a better choice than double-hung windows for this location; instead of wrenching your back to lift a sash, you simply turn a crank. These windows allow Alec and Ken to look out to the street in the morning and feel a part of the neighborhood as they watch the world go by.

Island Living

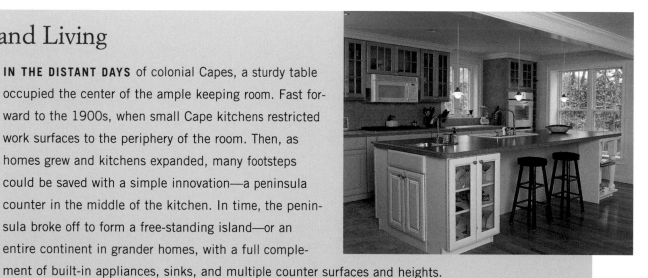

CAPE DETAILS

☆ **IN THE DISTANT DAYS** of colonial Capes, a sturdy table occupied the center of the ample keeping room. Fast forward to the 1900s, when small Cape kitchens restricted work surfaces to the periphery of the room. Then, as homes grew and kitchens expanded, many footsteps could be saved with a simple innovation—a peninsula counter in the middle of the kitchen. In time, the peninsula broke off to form a free-standing island—or an entire continent in grander homes, with a full complement of built-in appliances, sinks, and multiple counter surfaces and heights.

With two sides from which to work, an island can be a real asset in a kitchen with more than one cook. But if your kitchen is narrower than 11 ft., an island probably will act more as a barrier than a convenience. You need to leave a minimum of 3 ft. between facing counters or appliances, and it's best to allow at least another 6 in. or 12 in.

While the kitchen was being enlarged, the undersize dining room bow window was transformed into a prominent bay with a new copper roof. Built-in corner cabinets continue the angle of the bay into the room, helping to integrate the window unit. The inner rear wall of the dining room was replaced with two pairs of columns that frame the hallway beyond. This is another house that is brought above the ordinary by its attention to the transition areas between rooms. A hollow-core door surrounded by clamshell molding is functional, but it tends to suggest that the spaces on either side are victims of a stingy budget.

The stairway in many Capes springs from the front entryway, so that anyone who comes downstairs is apt to run into guests at the door. The relocated stairway of this house delivers the family to the interior of the plan.

Perfectly Architectural

ABOVE, **This handsome wooden** gateway works as a second entrance to the home and grounds.

FACING PAGE, **Don't be timid** about using heavyweight trim for outdoor projects. Sturdy posts at the entrance to this deck give it a look of permanence and durability.

Bill and Julia are the third owners of this brick 1941 Cape in a Washington, D.C., suburb. Their development was originally promoted with a brochure that described "architecturally perfect homes in the medium price range." Bill and Julia's place is slightly above average, having been occupied by the developer. The embellishments include crown molding in the living and dining rooms that once graced the Superior Court Library. This developer certainly was ahead of his time in using salvaged materials.

But architecturally perfect the house was not—not after 60 years of use. Although it was in fine structural shape, in characteristic Cape fashion the rooms were small, the second floor had yet to be finished, and access to the backyard was minimal. The owners saw great potential for more living space in both the attic and the neglected sun porch off the kitchen.

Julia is an architect and had the advantage of being able to design and supervise this job while living on site. She began by coming up with a master plan, acknowledging that it would be implemented in stages as finances would permit. As it turned out, the changes you see here took eight years to complete.

ABOVE, **A new centered dormer** and impressive deck and arbor combine to redeem the rear elevation of this otherwise simple Cape.

RIGHT, **A new quarry tile floor** and a slate fireplace complete the renovations of this former unheated porch. The room's outer walls are made up of combination doors, with interchangeable screens and glass panels.

Setting the Stage

Bill and Julia began their series of renovations with the addition of a deck that spans the back of the house. Starting with an outside improvement might seem like putting the cart before the horse, but the deck made it easier for workers to install French doors in the dining room and sunroom.

A deck can look like an overgrown playpen when merely tacked up alongside a house. Julia artfully designed this one to include a wisteria-covered arbor of cedar. The arbor permits dappled sunlight to shine through the vines in the summer; in winter, the sun's rays can pass through to reach the windows and French doors. The deck was painted to match the trim of the house so that it would appear more like a genteel porch than a simple platform.

Julia considered the arrangement of the deck, arbor, and dormer overhead as parts of a single composition, although they are at the back of the house—a facade that typically receives little attention. Even the gate to the backyard was conceived with extraordinary care. It is something of a wooden monument to the importance the couple place on backyard living. As you plan a renovation or addition, consider how much time you spend sitting in your backyard; if it is a center of family life, then this side of the house should be treated as more than a surface pierced by windows and doors.

A Suite for the Daughters

With the arrival of their first daughter, Bill and Julia decided to set aside a second-floor room as a nursery and add an adjacent bathroom. The balance of the sec-

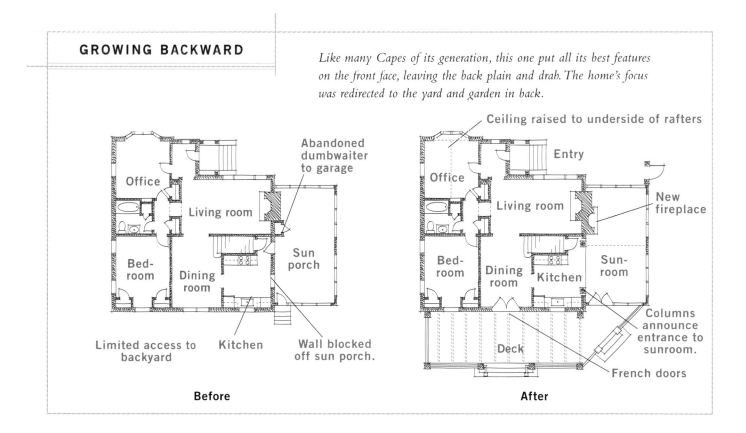

GROWING BACKWARD

Like many Capes of its generation, this one put all its best features on the front face, leaving the back plain and drab. The home's focus was redirected to the yard and garden in back.

Before

Office
Living room
Bedroom
Dining room
Kitchen
Sun porch
Abandoned dumbwaiter to garage
Limited access to backyard
Wall blocked off sun porch.

After

Office
Living room
Bedroom
Dining room
Kitchen
Sun-room
Deck
Ceiling raised to underside of rafters
Entry
New fireplace
Columns announce entrance to sunroom.
French doors

LEFT, **When entwined with vines,** an overhead arbor will shield the area below from the summer sun's rays, while allowing the low winter sun to come through after the foliage dies back.

FACING PAGE, **A clear view** into the sunroom from the kitchen helps keep cooks and the pots-and-pans crew from feeling isolated. Floor-level changes can be dangerous; here, the step is advertised by the sturdy-looking columns and a switch in floor materials.

chase⁓A vertical conduit or passageway in which wiring, plumbing, and heating lines are run.

ond floor was left as an open loft. The nursery has a special kid's-eye-view opening looking down into Julia's office below. This interior window was fitted with a ½-in.-thick acrylic panel to prevent falls.

Although bathrooms usually are stacked above one another for the sake of efficiency, this isn't a rigid rule. Here, Julia chose to locate a new second-floor bath in a wide gable dormer immediately above the dining room, but not far from the plumbing lines in the kitchen. The new dormer added a handsome architectural element to the rear elevation of the house. It is subtly ornamented with recessed panels, as are the posts for the new arbor and gateway.

The old sun porch had been used for years as the home's unofficial catch-all space, and it suffered from neglect. This seemed to be the ideal spot for a family room—just off the kitchen and accessible to the back deck. A dumbwaiter shaft, originally built to haul groceries and firewood up from the garage, could be made over as both a **chase** for ductwork and a flue for the fireplace that Bill and Julia wanted to install.

The wall between the kitchen and the sun porch was completely removed and the opening spanned by a steel beam. The columns that frame the opening are decorative. They don't really hold up the house, but serve as a visual signal that there is a step down from the kitchen. The owners elected to retain the original combination glass-and-screen doors that formed the

A Setting for the Home

☆ **IF, LIKE MANY CAPE OWNERS**, you were drawn by a sunny yard and friendly neighborhood, you may find yourself investing the same care into planning the outside features as you do the house itself. Some fencing and pavement materials lend themselves to Capes better than others.

As the adage goes, strong fences make good neighbors, and a classic white picket fence is always an appropriate choice for a lawn-defining boundary. Picket fences go back to the earliest Capes (when they also may have served to prevent drifting sands from encroaching on the settlers' gardens). Another traditional wood fence choice is the post and rail, which can be made of sawn lumber or simple round posts with split rails.

Low fences, especially, can make good neighbors. If you build a fence no higher than 36 in., the folks on the other side will be able to see over it easily, and they won't feel confined or shut out.

Blacktop and concrete weren't a part of the colonial American landscape, of course. You may want to give some thought to paving types that won't be an affront to the house—randomly placed stepping-stones, brick, and flagstone. And consider alternatives to running the driveway and walks in arrow-straight lines. By building in gradual curves, you can suggest a slower, more gracious way of life.

A symmetrical, centered room
tends to have a quiet sense to it,
as with this dining room. This just
feels like the sort of space that
fosters good conversations.

perimeter walls, even though they are not insulated.
Together, the home's hot-air heating system and new
fireplace provide sufficient heat for the room.

Razing the Ceilings

Julia and Bill wanted to expand the sense of volume
throughout the house, and not only by following the
lines of the roof on the second floor. They took out the
sunroom's deteriorating drywall ceiling to reveal the
rafters and then removed the ceiling from Julia's wood-
paneled office, located in the single-story ell overlooking the street. A system of high-tech halogen lights calls
attention to the lofty spaces of the office.

In the process of removing its ceiling, the couple revealed not only the joists and rafters but also a quaint, diamond-shaped window in the gable that had been visible only from outside the house. Because the window was located above the study's ceiling, it had served merely as a decorative element for the exterior—an oddity that had bothered Julia. Now the office has a pair of distinctively shaped windows, one looking up into the children's bedroom and the other offering a view of the treetops. The kids can play upstairs while keeping an eye on Mom, and at night the diamond-shaped window glows from the lights within.

A home can be remodeled with two themes, one more modern and risk taking than the other. In this house, the dining room serves as a sort of stylistic anchor. It retains a traditional appearance, with understated wainscoting, the rescued crown molding, and stained French doors that make a visual connection with the sunroom. The rooms of a house will vary in the energy they seem to put off, and you may want to consider whether spaces should be vitalizing or relaxing as you plan your own renovation.

ABOVE, **A diamond-shaped window** (just visible at top) was exposed when the drywall ceiling in this room was removed. New lighting was affixed to the exposed ceiling joists.

LEFT, **Homeowners don't often** include interior windows when sketching ideas for a renovation, but this feature can do a lot to make a house seem more spacious. Members of the household tend to feel connected as well. This gothic-shaped window in the children's play area looks down into their mother's first-floor office, with its diamond-shaped window.

CHAPTER THREE

AMBITIOUS ADDITIONS

Can't grow to the sides? Don't want to fill up the backyard with house? Then grow up! This two-story addition greatly increased the living space of the little brick Cape without eating up much of the small lot.

W HILE THE AVERAGE AMERICAN HOUSEHOLD has gotten smaller since World War II, the average American home has grown bigger. Unaltered postwar Capes now look tiny in comparison. Even small families have come to expect more space than a standard-issue six-room Cape offers, including individual bedrooms for two or more kids, perhaps a home office, and a family room.

If this is your situation, you may choose to stay put and go through the short-term (but intense) disruption of a major construction project, rather than "trade up" to a larger house. Perhaps your family has developed an affection for its little Cape. Or it could be that you appreciate living in an affordable, close-knit neighborhood that is within a walk or drive of work, school, and shops.

Fortunately for Cape owners, the style is malleable, and agreeably so. For proof of that, you need only drive through a 1950s neighborhood in which once-identical Capes now display their owners' individual additions

This neatly tailored Cape started its life as an undistinguished Ranch.

ABOVE, **Even the plainest of Capes** has the potential to blossom into a home of a very different sort. This one went through a romantic makeover, with a swooping roof and projecting gables.

BELOW, **This Cape is a tangible timeline** of history. The original, largest section was built in the 1700s. Over the years, the quest for more daylight (not to mention more space) led to grafting on dormers and an addition with large windows.

and modification. In the original Levittowns, just a handful of untouched houses remain.

There is no rule about what works and what does not when it comes to adding on—except this one, perhaps. Never be the *biggest* house on the block, especially on a block of modest homes. Otherwise, you run the risk of living in a white elephant that just doesn't fit into the suburban landscape. Instead, aim for the quiet goal of being the *best*. Put quality of design first, rather than seeing how many new rooms your budget will accommodate. Your house certainly will be distinctive in its new form, but without tearing the fabric of the neighborhood.

A Marriage of New and Old

If you live in a historic Cape, the challenge is a little more involved. You not only should take care that the house doesn't seem incongruous but also should design the new work so that it fits in with the house itself. The trick is to be considerate of the old while feeling free to redefine the contemporary. As with a precious

Living in a historic house can lead to a mild case of claustrophobia, with low ceilings and teeny windows. This sunroom was added as a counterpoint to that legacy. It is respectfully tucked in behind the older part of the house and uses similar materials so it blends in.

Renovation, Restoration, and Reproduction

THE CHANGES that we make to a house can usually be classified in one of three ways, depending on our intentions.

In renovation, broken or compromised portions of an older house are replaced or obliterated altogether with little regard for maintaining historical significance. Although there rarely is concern about a preserving a home's history if it is only a couple of decades old, even postwar Capes might have nostalgic details that are worth preserving.

Restoration usually involves structures that have some historical value. Damaged components are repaired and preserved; original portions are left intact or made good as new. For example, restoration proponents will opt to rebuild a crumbling 1700s chimney with the original bricks, whereas a renovator may achieve an antique look with contemporary materials.

Reproduction is a simulation of an origi-

nal. While it is possible to reproduce an "antique" original, you may find it more interesting (and more fruitful) to build a new house that interprets original Capes rather than getting the look down to the last square-headed nail.

antique, much of the charm of an old house is in the patina; attempts to buff up those gently sagging, tawny-edged rooms may erase their priceless aura. Your choices of architect and contractor are key here. At the same time, now is your chance to boldly shape a space suited to the quirks and habits of your family—perhaps a once-in-a-lifetime chance. With this much riding on a major remodeling, it's best to consult with people who have experience with older homes and the problems special to them.

An addition to an antique house doesn't have to have a strong family resemblance. In fact, it can be extremely difficult to make exact matches in materials between old and new, and you may be better off making

a clear switch in roofing and siding; a slight variation is apt to be annoying, rather than vitalizing. Instead, you can celebrate the differences between the original and the new work. One way to do this is to let the old part remain more prominent so that it continues to set the theme; make the added portion less conspicuous by keeping it smaller or stepping it back. Another way to respect the older home's integrity is to link it to the new work with a small transitional structure, so that the two halves of the house remain distinct.

As an owner of an antique Cape, you might find that you crave daylight and open spaces as an antidote to the somewhat dark or constricted interior you've been living in. Over the years, the 1763 Connecticut Cape shown in the bottom photo on p. 88 was enlarged with a dormer and a kitchen addition and then carefully and lovingly restored. But, keeping true to its historic style, the oldest rooms were dim and pinched, with small windows and low ceilings. To counterbalance all that quaintness, the owner wanted a bright sunroom in which to enjoy the beautiful property and natural light (see the photo on p. 89).

The very notion of a sunroom seems foreign to a historic Cape, but architect Jay Bright was able to connect a sympathetic addition to the 1930s kitchen wing. By placing the addition at right angles to the main house, there is a clear boundary between old and new. It projects out into the backyard, with windows on three sides—not traditional double-hungs, but the new windows are patterned with small panes that refer back to the core house.

ABOVE, **A built-in banquette** under the window saves floor space, allowing the table to be pushed closer to the outside wall. The hanging light fixture's location can be adjusted to suit dining, board games, and other activities.

LEFT, **This clapboard Cape** in the Connecticut woods expanded by reaching for the sky. A new second floor was added above the white beltline.

Tight lot restrictions influenced the redesign of this suburban Connecticut Cape. The house grew in height, but very little in its footprint, keeping the design lean and tall (see the floor plans below). Through it all, the house retains its Cape roots.

Stretching Out and Up

Often, a large addition comes about only after a lot of deferred planning and not until the growing family faces having to place bunkbeds in the hall. Adding significant volume to any house is accomplished by either going out or going up—or both. A basic Cape, with its simple roof slopes and straightforward gable ends, invites either approach. So, it's often the case that the limitations of the lot will determine the direction of the project. In a typical Cape neighborhood with closely spaced houses, a narrow lot tends to preclude a side addition, and a small backyard suggests tucking an addition close to the house.

If you're like most of us, cost is another factor influencing your choices, of course. Foundations are pricey, so if a new room can be built above an existing one

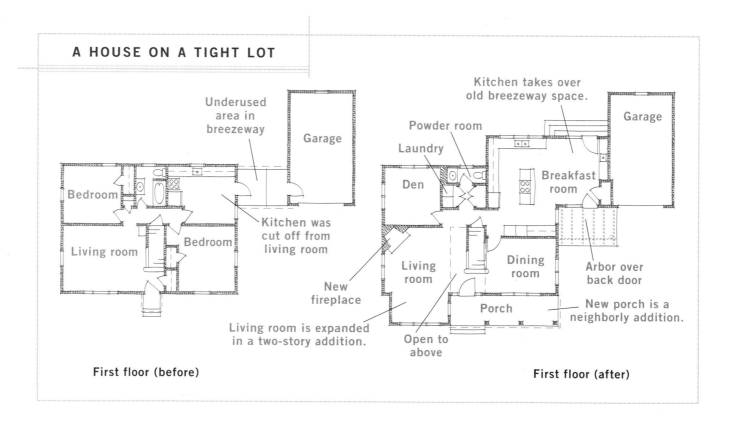

A HOUSE ON A TIGHT LOT

Underused area in breezeway

Garage

Bedroom

Kitchen was cut off from living room

Living room

Bedroom

New fireplace

Living room is expanded in a two-story addition.

First floor (before)

Kitchen takes over old breezeway space.

Powder room

Laundry

Den

Garage

Breakfast room

Living room

Dining room

Arbor over back door

Porch

New porch is a neighborly addition.

Open to above

First floor (after)

Influenced by the old Dutch Colonial homes of the region, this house has a gambrel roof— or the appearance of one. In fact, the double-pitched roof is merely an add-on to a simply framed second story. The original house is shown at left.

Domesticity and the natural
world—the room of this Cape
offers both, with a crackling fire
and a wall of windows looking
down to a river view.

(assuming that the structure can support it), you spare
the expense of building from the ground up. Or you
may choose to have a two-story addition rather than
planning a one-story addition with a foundation of
twice the size.

The placement of an addition also may be influenced
by the type of living space you're after. Rooms for
entertaining and gathering are usually placed on the
ground floor, with access to the outdoors and plenty of
windows. Conversely, bedrooms require privacy, security,
and some degree of distance from the hustle and bustle
of an active household, and they customarily are placed
upstairs in a Cape (although recent renovations often
feature a ground-floor master bedroom). There's no reason you can't stand a house on its head, of course, with
these positions reversed, and that's an option to keep in
mind in the early stages of brainstorming.

MANY MINOR CHANGES

In another mental twist, you can approach a tight budget and a tight lot as *opportunities* rather than obstacles,
and in doing so end up with a solution that delights
the eye as well as meets your needs. Take a look at the
postwar Cape in suburban Connecticut shown in the
photo and floor plans on p. 92. Restricted by side setbacks within the property lines, this home made the
most of its assets and minimized its shortcomings
through a number of smaller changes that take place all
over the structure. If the addition of your dreams
threatens to barge over into the neighbor's lot, then it's
time to fine-tune what you've got rather than make a
single bold move.

The Cape on p. 92 was transformed by architect Gary deWolf into a spacious three-bedroom house with two-and-a-half baths, involving only limited additions to the footprint at the front and back. The project turned a little-used breezeway into living space and created a full second floor by raising the roof all around. Inside, walls were shifted and rooms were reassigned to meet the owner's requirements. In this way, the architect was able to accomplish all of the owner's objectives without building much beyond the walls.

The Morphed Cape

As charming as Capes may be, some owners choose to reconceive them in other styles from other times. If you are considering a major expansion, you might allow yourself to imagine your home as a two-story Colonial farmhouse or a picturesque Bungalow. It is possible to transform a house so completely that no one would guess it once was a Cape—if that is your intention.

Even very early on, Capes began changing according to their owners' means and the architectural trends of the day—they grew rooms and borrowed ornament

ABOVE, **An archway frames** the opening between a master bedroom and adjoining sitting area. Just above the bench is a smaller arch, framing a niche for treasured objets d'art.

LEFT, **This clapboard octagon** sunroom was added to a Royal Barry Wills Cape.

stick framing — A contemporary building system that uses thin pieces of lumber to construct the frame, in contrast to the heavy members used in post-and-beam work.

FACING PAGE AND BELOW,
The front of this waterside home faces the water, but its standard Cape layout didn't take full advantage of the spectacular view. The front was boldly removed altogether to add a year-round sun space.

from the larger, more fashionable Federal and Greek Revival styles. Later, indoor plumbing had its effect on the Cape's floor plan. By the early 1950s, central heating, **stick framing,** and premanufactured doors and windows were the norm. It seems that then, as now, homeowners tended to want a traditional-looking house from the street but were open to contemporary touches that weren't obvious to a passerby. In line with this idea, some Levittown houses featured large sliding glass doors in back and two-sided fireplaces inside, features that the Levitts admired in Frank Lloyd Wright's homes of the period.

Here again, you should consider the neighborhood surroundings and also the climate of the region before undertaking a transformation. A Cape remodeled into a moss-covered Spanish Colonial with a tile roof would

be fine for Georgia but might seem incongruous in Maine. To pick a less extreme example, Victorian gingerbread tacked onto a Cape looks inappropriate, both to the style and possibly to the nearby houses as well. Merely embellishing the exterior with symbols of a style will rarely add substance to a house—especially to a Cape, which has as a defining hallmark a conspicuous lack of gewgaws.

Opening a Cape to the Outdoors

To the original Cape dwellers, the elements presented a survival challenge. Windows were necessary for light but were kept relatively small and few to conserve heat. Today, with central heating and insulating glass, windows can be treated much more boldly. Without veering too far from tradition, you can gang together conventional **double-hungs** or casements to create the impression of a transparent wall. A window wall will admit a flood of sunlight, help warm the house, and ease the boundary between indoor and outdoor environments. You can also set large areas of glass into a

ABOVE, **A screened porch** needn't be a house-enfolding feature to be inviting. This one is just large enough for a table and chairs, and is used for al fresco dining.

RIGHT, **This small, prim arbor** forms a transition between indoors and outside. The open structure allows some sunlight to reach the house—at least until vines cloak it.

double-hung — A window with independently operating upper and lower sashes.

Although porches are not native to Capes, they look perfectly at home if constructed with line and materials consistent with the house. This porch is a real departure, set within the base of a new cross-gable addition.

wall, but a more sympathetic approach might be to use French doors, the tall muntined units adapted from Parisian apartment-style windows. These are an especially good choice when a deck or terrace abuts the house.

Sunrooms are our modern-day conservatories, surrounded on two or more sides by glass. They allow a year-round appreciation of the outside world but should be carefully oriented to the sun, based on your latitude; a lot of glazing can act as a passive solar heating system, which may be either welcome or a nuisance,

depending on the time of year. A house in a northern climate would benefit from a sunroom on the south side, although you might want the summertime shade of a deciduous tree to moderate the sun's rays. In more southern states, this feature might better be placed to the east so that it doesn't catch the full force of the midday sun. In the Deep South, a screened porch often is the preferred alternative.

A **climbing vine** graces a south-facing porch, providing welcome shade in summer.

ROOMS WITHOUT WALLS

For considerably less money and trouble than a sunroom, you can enjoy a shorter season with a deck, terrace, porch, arbor, or patio. If arranged with some care, this space can serve as an outdoor room, substantially increasing the livable area of the home during warmer months. But if placed in an inhospitable spot—in full, day-long sun or overlooking a neighbor's yard—it may not see much use. Consider climate, exposure, and privacy when deciding what to put on your Cape and where to put it.

As with a sunroom, a south-facing deck or terrace is best when it has some degree of shade. A fringe of tree limbs or an overhead arbor will filter the sun's force and make a pleasantly sun-dappled spot for even hot days; a traditionally styled arbor will fit in particularly well with a Cape. Come autumn, the sun's angle is lower

Outdoor Showers

CAPE DETAILS

THE CAPE COD HOUSE has spread far from its origins on a sandy spit of land in the Atlantic, of course; but a good number of renovated and brand new Capes seem to be along the shore, and outdoor shower stalls have become a common accessory. Even if your home's body of water is a chlorinated pool, it's convenient (and pleasant) to be able to rinse off before going inside. The basic components are a shower valve and faucet that can be shut off and drained during freezing months, and a small enclosure for privacy. If the neighbors' house is close by, check that there won't be a line of sight from their top-floor windows. The enclosure doesn't have to call attention to itself, if it's treated as a tiny extension of the house rather than as a feature.

Washing the dog, scrubbing dusty planters, and doing other outside chores are less unpleasant if hot water is on tap.

and it will reach through the leafless branches to warm the flagstones and penetrate the windows beyond. An open or screened porch, on the other hand, is most delightful when shaded by the rest of the house or by surrounding trees. It relies on summer winds for cooling and may be best located on the breezy side of your house. Although early Capes weren't typically built with porches, a modest size one won't look like an aberration if it is trimmed similarly to the home.

A disastrous fire took the heart out of this Cape but left the stone walls standing as a start on an ambitious rebuilding. The oldest section of this house, the left-hand wing, dates back to the 1700s. (The top photo on the facing page shows the porch up close.)

From Cape to Colonial

French doors are a good way to isolate a room acoustically while maintaining a visual connection. And, of course, they also let light filter through from one space to another.

hip roof — A roof with slopes at both sides and both ends.

cornice — The horizontal trim above a window or doorway.

JOHN AND JILLIAN WERE EXPECTING THEIR SECOND daughter when they began work on their Cape. They had no attachment to its essential Capeness, and so there wasn't anything to keep them from ripping off the old roof and constructing an entirely new second floor with 8-ft. ceilings.

They worked with architect Tucker Chase to design a front porch that would add more than a dash of style. Beneath its **hip roof** the painted floorboards and beadboard ceiling create an anteroom, hinting at living spaces within. The hip roof permits the gutter downspouts to drop down the face of the house, a less conspicuous location than along the face of the porch posts. The porch doubles as a front hall in the warmer weather, a place to greet guests and leave umbrellas. Beyond the new porch, the built-up **cornices** at the window heads and symmetrical window locations on the front facade turned this humble little Cape into a dressed-up Colonial.

Up top, the new roof crowning this Cape turned Colonial has a steep pitch, about 12-in-12. The architect at first had suggested a shallower pitch, but Jillian wanted their new roof to retain the characteristic steep

The simple, clean lines of this porch are played up by the new paint job—particularly the glossy floor. Beadboard provides a more interesting ceiling than would have been had with plywood.

The little house that grew. This traditional-looking Colonial started out as a Cape, but the second-story addition doubled its square footage. The front porch conceals the asymmetrical window and door arrangement at the first floor, helping to balance the composition.

pitch from its traditional look. There was a practical concern, too. Although a shallow-pitched roof is cheaper to build, it wouldn't allow the ample storage space offered by the original attic.

Looking at the house from the street, the effect is as if the house had been lifted off the ground so that a new first floor could be inserted. The footprint was increased only by the area of the front porch, allowing the project to conform easily to the local zoning code.

John and Jillian's house had a three-season back porch running the entire width of the Cape. In theory, a porch is a cheery place, but this one seemed rather a gloomy place instead, and the new front porch was seeing all the use. It was a small sacrifice to give up the

The kitchen cabinets were reused from the original kitchen. The contrast of black hardware against the white cabinets creates a pleasing graphic composition alongside the unmistakably modern-looking stainless-steel appliances.

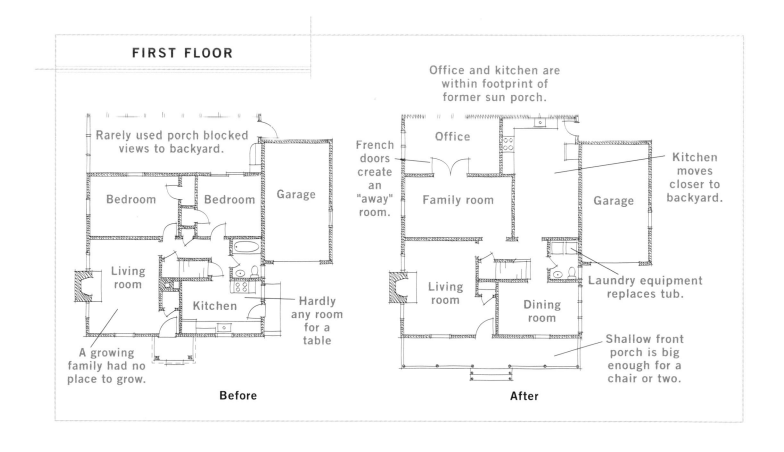

FIRST FLOOR

Rarely used porch blocked views to backyard.

Bedroom

Bedroom

Garage

Living room

Kitchen

Hardly any room for a table

A growing family had no place to grow.

Before

Office and kitchen are within footprint of former sun porch.

Office

French doors create an "away" room.

Family room

Garage

Kitchen moves closer to backyard.

Living room

Dining room

Laundry equipment replaces tub.

Shallow front porch is big enough for a chair or two.

After

A large bathroom in a small house is an extravagance, but one that is justified considering how much time you might spend in there. You don't necessarily have to buy high-ticket fixtures; roomy proportions and large windows contribute to the sense of luxury.

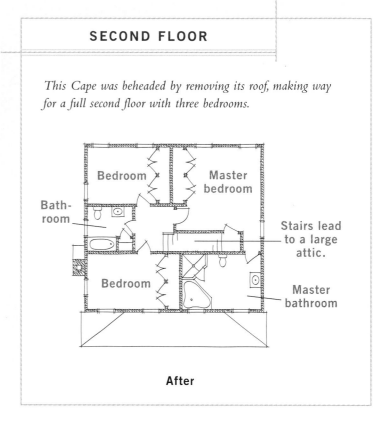

SECOND FLOOR

This Cape was beheaded by removing its roof, making way for a full second floor with three bedrooms.

Bedroom

Master bedroom

Bath-room

Stairs lead to a large attic.

Bedroom

Master bathroom

After

back porch to extend the outer limits of the house onto the existing slab.

The kitchen now occupies half of the former porch and also reaches into the heart of the house, for overall dimensions that allow room for a large family dining table. Jillian and John opted to recycle the old kitchen cabinets, sprucing them up with a fresh coat of paint and splurging on stainless-steel appliances for contrast. Up front, the former kitchen is now a dining room that overlooks the front porch. The living room remains in its original location just inside the front door, but in pleasant weather it takes on a more expansive feeling with the new porch just outside the front door.

Alongside the kitchen at the back of the first floor is a family room separated from the new office by a pair

of French doors. Jillian works from home, and from her desk she can keep an eye on her children whether they are in the family room or on the backyard swing set.

Upstairs, the once-cramped attic has been transformed with a very efficient floor plan that includes three sunny bedrooms and two baths. The ceilings are 8 ft. high throughout. The master bath is the size of many small bedrooms and includes both a shower stall and a deep spa tub, perfect for bubble baths for John and Jillian's two daughters. The dove-gray walls moderate the stark black-and-white geometry of the floor. The girls have their own bathroom tucked between their bedrooms. One of the benefits of a Cape, with its relatively small footprint, is that the bathrooms almost always have a window, rather than being buried deep within a complex layout.

To trim or not to trim? In many Cape upgrades, the plain rooms of a newer house are fitted with traditional molding, but you may choose to go easy on the trim in the modern fashion. And sometimes trim just isn't practicable. In this room, crown molding of any size would have rubbed shoulders with casing around the opening to the hall.

From Cape to Bungalow

ABOVE, **A hutch and paneled wainscoting** give historical accents to a bare-bones room with no traditional associations of its own.

FACING PAGE, **You can spot** the profile of the original Cape that is now masquerading as a Bungalow. Bungalows typically have front porches, lending them a neighborly aspect.

IN CONTRAST TO THEIR NEIGHBORS UP THE STREET (see pp. 102–107), Sue and Steve preferred to maintain the cottagelike aspect of their house. Architect Gary deWolf's solution was to leave the roof ridge intact, adding dormers and extending the roof to incorporate a front porch in a way that makes the house look something like a Bungalow—a story-and-a-half style that became extremely popular in the early 1900s. The homes were characterized by a shallow-pitched roof that swept down to incorporate an inset porch. Dormers served to make the most of the low spaces on the second floor, and they formed snug alcoves for beds or desks.

In the front of this house, the two shed dormers, each with three small awning windows, peek out over the roof of the new porch. At the rear, a wide shed dormer cantilevers out over the original back wall, increasing the floor area enough to add a third bedroom and two full bathrooms. The dormers are supplemented by an unusually large double-hung window in each of the gable-end walls, improving ventilation and serving as the means of egress in the event of a fire.

Even if your kitchen becomes landlocked as the result of an addition, the sink can still take in a view if it is positioned on an island or a peninsula like this one.

Downstairs, the rooms kept their original locations, but the kitchen received a good deal of attention. It has been treated to a tile floor, a bank of new windows, new cabinets, and a peninsula with a granite countertop and stools alongside. This is now the best place to hang out at a party, chatting and snacking while keeping the cook company. The small dining room is reserved for quiet dinners away from the kitchen's clatter. A built-in hutch and wainscoting were added during the renovation to elevate the room beyond four plain walls.

The project took full advantage of the yard. There is a traditionally detailed front porch with crisp-painted white woodwork that matches the two rockers and a

Curtains on a porch? Yes, if the neighbors tend to frequent their own porch or patio when you happen to be lounging. Curtains or blinds can also help moderate the power of the sun at certain times of the day.

IN THE BUNGALOW STYLE

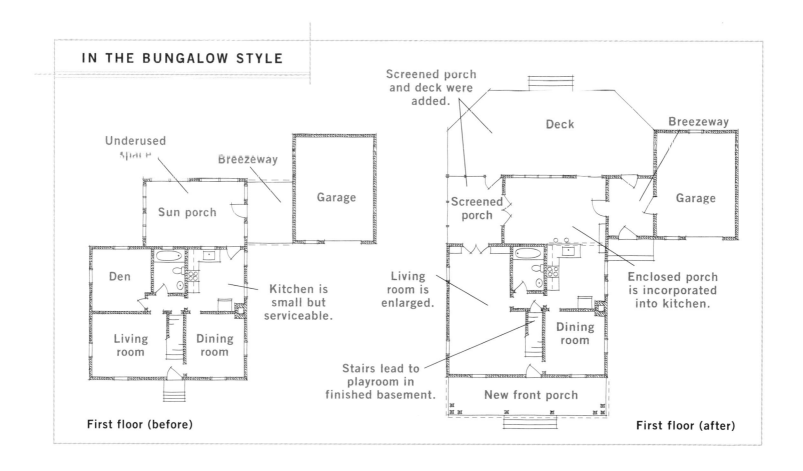

Underused space

Breezeway

Garage

Sun porch

Den

Kitchen is small but serviceable.

Living room

Dining room

First floor (before)

Screened porch and deck were added.

Deck

Breezeway

Screened porch

Garage

Living room is enlarged.

Enclosed porch is incorporated into kitchen.

Dining room

Stairs lead to playroom in finished basement.

New front porch

First floor (after)

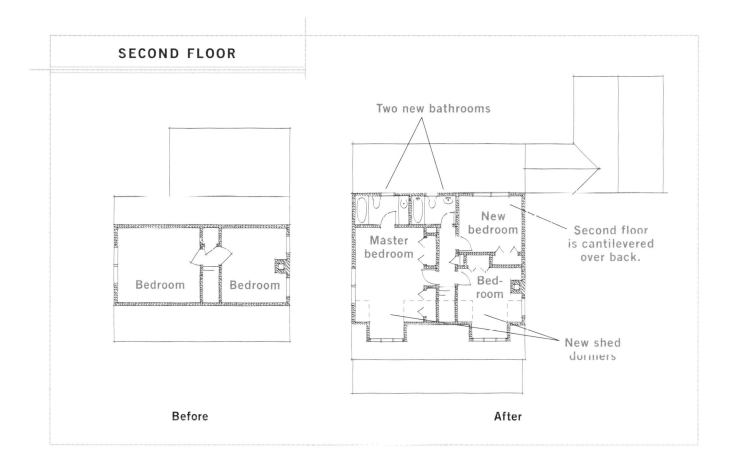

SECOND FLOOR

Two new bathrooms

Master bedroom

New bedroom

Bed-room

Second floor is cantilevered over back.

New shed dormers

Bedroom

Bedroom

Before

After

In postwar Capes, the dining room, if there is one, rarely accommodates more than six around the table. A renovation or addition offers the chance to provide a longish room that will allow for a full-size table and maybe a smaller one for the kids as well.

porch swing. Gary used three square posts to accentuate the corners and give the porch more definition.

For a bit of privacy, as well as protection from mosquitoes, the family can retreat to the rear screened porch. The second-floor framing is cantilevered to form the flat part of the porch ceiling. A large back deck is nestled into the corner created by the back of the house and the garage alongside. The deck serves as a transitional space between the house and the stone terrace a few steps down. The decking and the handrails were treated with a stain that tones down the wood and helps integrate this feature with the landscape. Unless you have some reason to play up the architecture of a deck, you may want to help it blend in with either the

A Tale of Two Neighbors

TAKE A WALK in a Cape-filled postwar neighborhood like Levittown, and you'll see the many ways that owners have transformed the little houses in their own personal vision. This suburban Connecticut neighborhood offers a textbook example of how two neighboring Capes (p. 102 and p. 108), nearly identical when built in the 1940s, have been remade into bright new homes. Each house began with a typical floor plan—four rooms gathered around a stairway leading to a dim, unfinished attic space upstairs. These houses had been fine for the two young married couples who lived there—until the stork arrived.

Working with different architects, the couples both requested three bedrooms and two baths upstairs, a family-size kitchen below, and a front porch. Porches make good sense in this neighborhood because of its open,

friendly nature—with kids free to roam through the unfenced yards. The difference between these renovation scenarios is that John and Jillian had a Colonial-style house in mind, whereas Sue and Steve were Bungalow-lovers at heart.

house (perhaps by taking a color from the trim) or with plantings. Cedar becomes less conspicuous over time, without your help, as it weathers. A grayish stain can be used to take the edge off the deck's newness.

A Natural Fit

This house began like all the others in the neighborhood—small and undistinguished Capes built fast and cheaply. Now, some 55 years later, the block has

matured into a row of individual personalities. The rhythm of the streetscape is still intact, largely because the side yards between each house have remained much the same, thanks to zoning restrictions that limit the breadth of the footprint. Laws of this sort can seem confining at times, but they do help ensure that houses stay compatible in scale and suited to the size of their lots.

Hidden from the street, this spacious deck is built in such a way
that it seems a part of the landscape.

A Spirited Transformation

ABOVE, **Twin columns** stand sentry, marking the doorway to the living room and continuing the design vocabulary initiated at the porch's colonnade through to the dining room entrance.

FACING PAGE, **A smaller version** of the front porch's columns is repeated atop the low partition separating the dining room from the living room. Round columns are classically elegant and serve as decorative features as well as functional components.

Y OU STILL CAN FIND SMALL, AFFORDABLE CAPES in desirable communities, but it takes a bit of imagination to convert one of these plain shoeboxes into a distinctive home. When Kris and Donna bought this little Cape in an established outer suburb of Boston, it was rather plain on the surface, with a "taut skin" as their architect, Paul Mahoney, put it. The flat facades offered almost no relief—nothing that animated the appearance, save for a box bay window in the living room. From the start, Paul proposed to activate each elevation with elements that would ornament the surface in a three-dimensional way.

A new front porch was not in Kris and Donna's plans when they asked Paul to redesign their home. But Paul explained that swapping the paltry stoop for a substantial porch would do a great deal to make something special of the highly visible front elevation. This would be seen as a neighborly gesture, too, making their sunny front yard all the more inviting for the kids along the street.

The porch decking is mahogany, a wood that has an expensive look but in fact costs just a little more than the typical cedar decking. Painted rails and balusters

This Cape reaches out to the world with a series of dormers and a broad front porch. The central dormer is an interesting hybrid of two hip dormers joined by a shed, adding to the interest of the profile the home holds up to the sky. The original house is shown at right.

link the wood columns and create a rhythm that high-lights the front steps; doubled columns signal the entrance. The porch is quite shallow—only 6 ft. from its front edge to the wall of the house—and this permits the low-angled winter sun to reach into the house.

Beyond Boxiness

A common goal in transforming a developer's house is to get away from the sense that the rooms are just a "series of boxy spaces," in Paul's words. Even though the living room was graced with a fireplace and the dining room had lovely paneled wainscoting, the door-ways into them were nothing more than simple cased openings with indifferent trim. To convert the rooms into a suite for entertaining, Paul removed the partition dividing them and installed a beam that spans the open-ing and is concealed within a foot-wide dropped **soffit.** The view into the dining room and the window beyond is now symmetrically framed by two low walls topped with pairs of Tuscan-style wooden columns that support the soffit.

The columns aren't an isolated feature, but have been used elsewhere in the house. The new opening between the living room and foyer is framed by two full-height columns under a similar soffit. Now, upon entering the front door there is a long, space-expanding diagonal view from the entry hall to the far corner of the dining room. Although the rooms remain distinct, they have a more transparent reading at their edges, and the layout no longer comes across as isolated cubicles.

Kris and Donna were planning to keep the fireplace, but even attractive features sometimes have to be sacri-ficed for the larger good of a whole-house reconfigura-tion. Its corner location made furnishing the living room difficult, and the couple wanted a more spacious

FIRST FLOOR

The exterior of this Cape wasn't much to look at. The new scheme perks up the house with hip-roofed dormers and a front porch, while creating more living space.

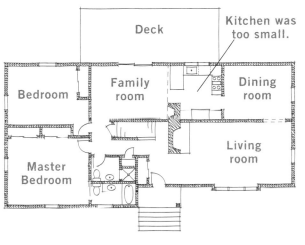

Before

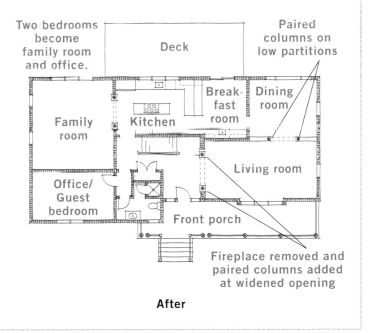

After

soffit — The underside of the trim running under the eaves; the flat, dropped portion of ceiling at a beam or at the perimeter of a room.

Kitchen Candlepower

NOTHING IS MORE FRUSTRATING than working in a dimly lit kitchen, so lighting should be considered early on in the design process. Natural light is important, especially in the morning, and it's best to make the most of eastern-facing kitchen windows. At sundown, you need a combination of ambient, or general lighting, and task, or focused lighting. With a combination of both—and dimmer switches—you'll be able to change the feel of the kitchen dramatically for different occasions.

Recessed lights and unobtrusive ceiling-mounted fixtures are good choices for style-neutral ambient lighting, especially in a low-ceiling Cape kitchen. A decorative pendant fixture over the table or island can be used as a design feature that focuses light on the activity rather than the ceiling. And if the fixture is of a somewhat historical style, it can help suggest a Colonial-era theme for an otherwise unapologetically modern kitchen.

connection between this room and the entry hall. To make this loss easier to take, there is now a new fireplace on the drawing board for the family room.

Family-Size Spaces

Occasionally, the shape of a room works against its function, so that it is better to come up with a new use for the space. At the back of this house, a long and fairly narrow family room always had seemed somewhat inhospitable. Paul converted it into a generous-size kitchen and breakfast room; they connect to the new family room via another column-flanked portal. Kris and Donna wanted to carve a new family room out of former bedrooms, but again this would have yielded a space that didn't quite measure up. Paul convinced them to borrow a bit of room from Kris's home office,

and now the new room is big enough for the couple and their two sons to stretch out.

The kitchen's old-fashioned tin ceiling was Kris's idea. In his job as a real estate developer, he had come across the material and wanted to give it a try. Originally, he and Donna intended to mute the surface by painting the tiles after installation, leaving just the texture of the tiles to catch the eye. But they liked the cheerful way the shiny ceiling bounced light around the kitchen and kept it as is.

The casement windows over the kitchen sink are uninterrupted by muntins, allowing a clear view of the backyard. Sunlight is reflected around the room by the shiny tin ceiling.

The eaves of this room were pushed toward the wall for more space, as marked by the change in direction of the floorboards. Kneewalls need only be high enough to tuck a bureau or bed under; we don't normally walk or stand so close to walls that we need a full-height ceiling around the perimeter of the room.

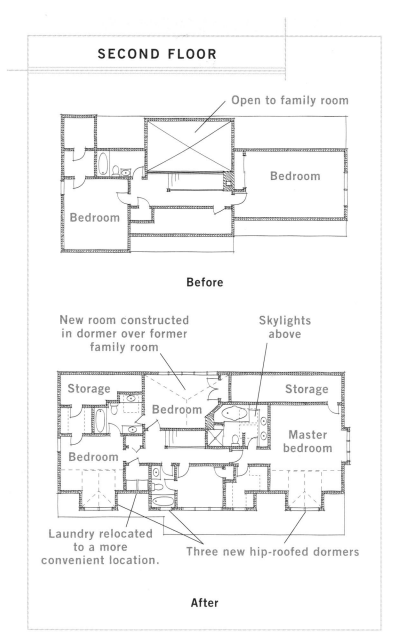

SECOND FLOOR

Open to family room

Bedroom

Bedroom

Before

New room constructed in dormer over former family room

Skylights above

Storage

Bedroom

Storage

Bedroom

Master bedroom

Laundry relocated to a more convenient location.

Three new hip-roofed dormers

After

Dormers Make the Difference

Upstairs, the floor plan was totally transformed. A pair of bedrooms and just one bath had been tucked under the ridge, without a dormer in sight. Paul designed three new hip-roofed dormers both to frame out more space and to create a different look for the house from the street.

The framing is different within each dormer, so they create distinct effects inside. In the master bedroom, the dormer forms a sunny alcove for a chaise lounge. In the child's room, a dropped beam cuts across the ceiling to make a cozy nook that's just the size of a twin bed.

In his work, Kris learned to be prepared for the serendipity that's inevitable in a remodeling project. He advises first-time remodelers to be willing to make changes as they go along, especially if theirs is an older house. If instead you try to be faithful to your blueprints, you're apt to miss out on the design opportunities that inevitably pop up during construction.

ABOVE, **Sometimes, a skylight** is better than a window. This operable skylight offers privacy, light, and ventilation.

LEFT, **This dormer** has an exposed beam that helps create a cozy space for a twin-size bed.

Trial Size to Family Size

ABOVE, **A parade of skylights** illuminates facing banks of closets in a hallway that links the existing house and the new master bedroom.

FACING PAGE, **The kitchen extends** into the family room with this inviting counter. The interior window to the left is a reminder of the original exterior wall of the house. It provides a view from the kitchen into the veranda.

WILLIAM AND KELLY PURCHASED THEIR 600-SQ.-FT. Cape in New Jersey before children came along, and its diminutive footprint and tiny rooms were just enough for a couple. It had all the necessary spaces, although just barely—living room, dining room, kitchen, and bath downstairs, with the second floor sliced into one larger and one smaller room.

The evolutionary path of this Cape unfolded as a series of phased additions. William, an architect, never conceived of a master plan with portions to be completed according to a schedule and a budget. Instead, whenever the family's needs became pressing and their finances improved, the house grew in a manageable burst.

Adding Volume

When daughter number one was due to arrive, the couple realized that they needed to build a master bedroom and bath upstairs—and fast. Originally, their plan was simply to finish out the second floor on the footprint they had. But ultimately, the project stretched out to capture additional volume—and challenge the envelope of the local zoning code. There eventually was a new two-car garage with a cupola-topped master

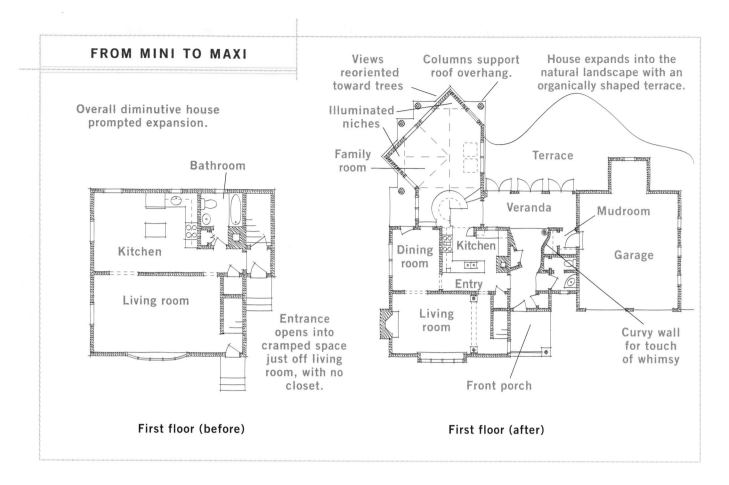

FROM MINI TO MAXI

Overall diminutive house prompted expansion.

Bathroom

Kitchen

Living room

Entrance opens into cramped space just off living room, with no closet.

First floor (before)

Views reoriented toward trees

Columns support roof overhang.

House expands into the natural landscape with an organically shaped terrace.

Illuminated niches

Family room

Terrace

Veranda

Mudroom

Dining room

Kitchen

Garage

Entry

Curvy wall for touch of whimsy

Living room

Front porch

First floor (after)

bedroom over it, and a ground-floor den linking the house with the garage.

Busy with a fledgling architectural practice, William's drawings for his own house were sketchy. Many of the details evolved on the fly during construction, such as the parade of skylights over the passage to the master bedroom. Headroom was tight because the new roof had to be married to the existing shed dormer at the back of the original house, so adding the skylights was a way to lighten the ceiling and slightly raise the headroom—to the face of the glass. The intervening ribs of doubled-up rafters are lower, but not so low as to be head bumpers.

The unusual copper hood over the casement window above the garage doors was also a happy afterthought. Wind-driven rain had been finding its way through the window, so William conceived of this highly ornamen-

tal solution. The flat-seam construction is borrowed from a similar detail on the family room roof, and the triangular shape of the hood ties in with the curious cupola roof just above.

Wavy Walls and Deliberate Views

The next phase of work quickly followed on the heels of the first addition. William and Kelly were desperate for a new kitchen and family room that would take advantage of their sylvan setting, as well as provide more room for their daughters, now numbering three. A mudroom and downstairs powder room were also on the menu.

The kitchen remained in the original spot, but it was renovated to include a round counter for eating. There was an effort to avoid synthetic materials throughout

ABOVE AND LEFT, This 2,200-sq.-ft. home for a family of five began life as a mini-Cape less than a third that size (shown at left).

The cupola over the bedroom has two functions: to provide a perky ornament for the addition, and to allow moonlight to sweep over the sleeping homeowners.

the project, and the couple chose simple maple cabinets topped with dark stone countertops and a wood floor rather than sheet vinyl.

The family room was angled to direct views toward a wooded glen rather than a neighbor's house directly in back. The room is a diverting geometric exercise, with angled protrusions at the corners and ceiling forms that call to mind the little roof on the cupola. Illuminated niches alternate with large windows and angled clerestories, filling the dynamic space with light. On the outside, this addition is decorated with a grid of panels, and columns support the roof overhang.

As the home evolved, not every new space was allowed to remain. A den that appeared in the first phase of construction later gave way to a new entry hall, mudroom, and powder room. And there was a

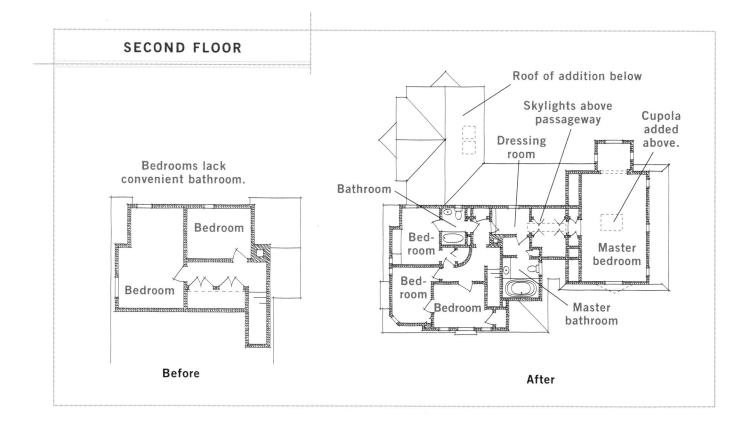

SECOND FLOOR

Bedrooms lack convenient bathroom.

Bedroom

Bedroom

Before

Roof of addition below

Skylights above passageway

Cupola added above.

Dressing room

Bathroom

Bed-room

Bed-room

Bedroom

Master bedroom

Master bathroom

After

The television sits in one of the protruding corners in a custom-designed cabinet. Lit from above, the unit is something of a focal point, much like a fireplace might be.

This wall throws a curve just for the simple delight of shaping space in an interesting way.

Porch Notes

☆ **THE ORIGINAL CAPES** weren't adorned with front porches, but they are a natural fit nevertheless. A porch can embellish the blank look of a standard postwar Cape. And for a family, a porch is a transitional space between outside and inside, with a more refined appearance than a deck.

The front porch may do double-duty as a foyer, since Capes are generally short on entry amenities. Traditional porches tended to be shallow in depth,

and 8 ft. should be plenty on a Cape, permitting the light to reach the windows of the rooms within. The time-honored flooring material is tongue-and-groove wood, painted or left natural; for the ceiling, you might use beadboard, with its more ornamental appearance. Porch ceilings usually were painted robin's egg blue. One explanation for this is that the color discourages flying insects from landing. Or it simply could be that people enjoy sitting under a sky-colored surface.

measure of whimsy. The entry features a distinctive wavy wall, punctuated with a column. "The curved wall is all about circulation," William explains. It playfully expresses that this particular area is a passageway, a place to move through.

The house is large enough that not every space has to serve a fixed purpose. The chameleon-like veranda finds a number of uses. With its brick floor and piers and three pairs of French doors, it serves as an indoor–outdoor room. The children can stretch out on the sun–warmed bricks for a board game or to play hopscotch on a rainy day. Because the dining room is large enough only for family dinners, William and Kelly bring out several round tables to accommodate larger gatherings. In the evening, with the French doors flung open, the veranda becomes a sidewalk café right inside their own home.

LEFT, **The circus theme** of this child's bedroom went beyond clown wallpaper. A fabric ceiling puts the crib under the big tent and has the added benefit of softening the acoustic properties of the room.

BELOW, **The veranda and room** within have more angles than a protractor. The brick wall is answered by the herringbone pattern of the floor. The wood floor just inside is truncated on a slant, an interior wall goes off in its own direction, and in a far corner there is a beamlike assemblage above the television.

Children's bedrooms were part of this phase of work. A suite of bedrooms was added above the original house, accommodated by new dormers over the new front porch. The nursery is softened with a ceiling cover of fabric, gathered in the center. Down below, a small front porch with a porch swing is tucked under the protection of the home's form and made to seem all the more secure by the massive corner post (see the photo at left on the facing page).

It would be a Herculean challenge to enlarge a house this much in one swoop—it now has 2,200 sq. ft. of space. If you have big ambitions, consult with an architect about ways in which the work can be accomplished in stages without undoing too much in the process. The original Capes were intended to be expanding structures, after all. With some foresight, you shouldn't have to waste many walls and windows along the way.

A Cape Compound

Long, directed views through the house help orient the guests and organize the spaces. Pilasters break up the wall planes into smaller segments, announcing intersections along the hallways.

B ROTHERS DON AND JOHN CO-OWN THIS VACA-tion Cape a block from the beach along the Delaware shore, having inherited it from their parents. The house sees a lot of use: three generations of the two branches of the family tree are sometimes there together. Although the structure was in fine shape over-all, it had been tarnished by the accumulated years of sand, storms, and grandchildren. As is often the case with vacation homes, the kitchen was shabby and the bedrooms just adequate. The floor plan was casual, at best; the family room could be reached only by travel-ing through the bathroom. And, also in common with beach homes, the screened porch was the real living room, used for eating and lounging and doubling as a sleeping porch for the grandchildren.

Architect Kevin Huelster of Westport, Connecticut, had worked with the brothers on projects up north and was asked to redesign this Cape. Kevin reshuffled the overall room arrangement to allow more bedrooms and baths, and he advocated adding a new addition off the back for a kitchen and family room.

Privacy is a scarce commodity when multiple fami-lies get together at vacation homes. Holiday life goes more smoothly if everyone isn't cheek by jowl. Kevin

The new addition created a small compound of pavilion-like structures behind the original Cape. Contrasting siding ensures that the new work distinctly stands out.

RIGHT, **The kitchen is the linking** element in the house's new scheme. Its facing islands are centered under a change in the ceiling plan, punctuated by skylights and ringed by a lower ceiling.

BELOW, **The architect** tucked in this bar along the way between the kitchen and the formal dining room. Stock cabinets and dark countertops are illuminated by a skylight overhead, a theme repeated throughout the new work.

reconfigured this home so the bedrooms aren't separated by mere frame walls but by spaces used as closets and hallways to ensure acoustic privacy, and bathrooms are scattered here and there for convenience. The result is something like a tiny seaside hotel for this extended family.

Rethinking the Beach House

This being a beach house, the transition between inside and outside took some special care. In the newly remodeled house—with its hardwood floors—salty beach gear and sand no longer would be tolerated. Kevin designed a separate pavilion, resembling a kiosk, to house chairs, umbrellas, and other beach apparatus, and there is now an outdoor shower within a small enclosure. Today, beach-goers can leave the beach behind them before stepping inside the house.

The addition in back fits in well because it uses materials found on the existing house. The new family room is clad with tongue-and-groove cedar siding to match the dormers on the Cape's front. The kitchen portion of the addition is done in painted clapboard to match the original siding. Inside, the new spaces are large and bright—a deliberate contrast to the woodsy house the family had grown up with. The family room is open to a soaring ceiling that's cut out along the ridge for a striking bank of skylights. There is nothing about the facade of the beach home to suggest that this modern, cleanly sculpted space is within. Screen doors, clerestory windows, and French doors also help open the family room to the sun and sky. Kevin wanted to build in a seaside atmosphere, and floors are finished with a translucent white stain that suggests the wood had been bleached by exposure to the elements.

As is appropriate to a summer place, the new kitchen is inviting, easy to maintain, and big enough for an extended family to get involved at mealtimes. There is nothing formal here—the family room is on the other side of the counter. A portion of this counter has been

There is nothing extraordinary about this dormered Cape to suggest the boldness with which the interior has been opened up.

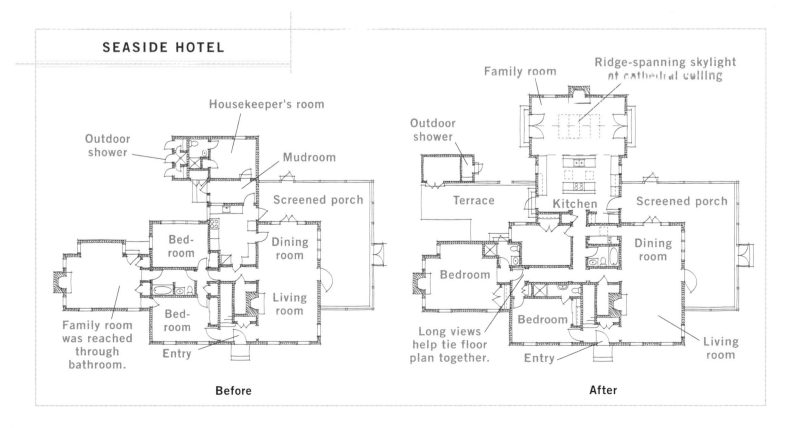

SEASIDE HOTEL

Before

- Outdoor shower
- Housekeeper's room
- Mudroom
- Screened porch
- Bedroom
- Dining room
- Living room
- Bedroom
- Family room was reached through bathroom.
- Entry

After

- Family room
- Ridge-spanning skylight at cathedral ceiling
- Outdoor shower
- Terrace
- Kitchen
- Screened porch
- Bedroom
- Dining room
- Long views help tie floor plan together.
- Bedroom
- Living room
- Entry

raised so that people can pull up stools for snacks or a light meal. Everything is light and bright, except for the nearby wet bar, with its natural-finished cabinets and black countertops. The bar area provides something of a transition into the quiet dining room beyond, with its exposed joists overhead, curtained windows, and traditional furniture. Both old and new coexist in this remodeling, allowing the family to keep in touch with their memories of past summers.

FACING PAGE AND ABOVE, **The strict geometry** of this family room structure implies a separate building, open to the sky and views in three directions. The skylight is dramatic, custom formed with steel framing that permits the ridge to be interrupted midspan.

House and Garden

retro guide

HISTORICALLY, Capes and other traditional homes placed the refined parlor and hall at the front of the house, while the more functional kitchen or keeping room was in the back. The yards adjacent to these rooms followed these relative levels of formality. Today, our houses still maintain a carefully landscaped front lawn for public viewing, and a more private and casual backyard that we actually inhabit. Beyond that, there are subtle things you can do to help ensure that your Cape looks at home on its lot.

Hardscaping elements, like fences, walkways, and light poles, should be selected to complement your Cape's cottage-like style. Wooden picket fences are more appropriate than chain link, to give an obvious example. A curved stone or brick pathway to the front door suits a Cape better than a straight shot of concrete sidewalk. As for landscaping, you might question the standard suburban formula of symmetrical foundation plantings forced into geometric shapes. A better solution might be to select an assortment of low-maintenance native plants placed to create a more natural-looking garden in the simple and refreshing cottage style.

A Cape for the Generations

ABOVE, **The seating area** in the hallway leading to the master bedroom is part library, part hallway. This intimate spot is a cozy getaway just down the hall from the family action in the main gathering spaces.

FACING PAGE, **To make this ambitious** project look modest in size, it was broken up into smaller segments. Each of the segments is similar in form to the original Half Cape.

BACK IN THE 1960s, BILL AND JO HIRED PAUL LANZA, a local builder, to construct a summer place just a short walk from the shore on Cape Cod. It was a classic Half Cape and very modest, with a living room in the front and a tiny galley kitchen, bath, and dining room in the back. In true Cape style, a narrow stairway climbed from the front entry, behind the living room's fireplace and chimney, to a single attic bedroom. The house's storybook scale and ageless detailing set the theme for the young couple's weekends at the beach. Sometime later, a breezeway was built between the house and new garage, and the second floor gained a rear shed dormer, but the place remained otherwise unchanged.

Fast-forward 30 years to find Bill and Jo back at the drawing board, this time working with Paul's son, Joe Lanza. Trained as an architect and as a master carpenter, Joe was charged with transforming the little cottage into a vacation home that would welcome four generations of the family and their assorted friends. The couple wanted four bedrooms for their clan, as well as a large gathering room. Because mealtimes were traditionally family events, the new kitchen would have a greatly expanded role. The challenge was to accomplish all this

Double skylights and windows on three sides bathe the new living room with light. The cabinet above the fireplace conceals a television. Wide-plank flooring was used throughout the house to unify its spaces, new and original.

without overwhelming—or even obliterating—the humble structure that meant so much to Bill and Jo. Joe Lanza set up shop in the garage and got to work.

A Family of Forms

Rather than merely attach a large, monolithic addition to the original Half Cape, Joe added on a series of room-size shapes. It's a strategy you'll see in other projects in the book—making the house look as though it had grown gradually and casually over the years, rather than in one major push.

No single part of the addition is larger than the original house, so that the existing structure sets the tone and the spirit. Like family members who resemble one another without being clones, each new section is distinguished by slightly different features—windows,

Because this house sits so low to the ground, the deck didn't require a perimeter guardrail and doesn't draw as much attention to itself as a feature of the home.

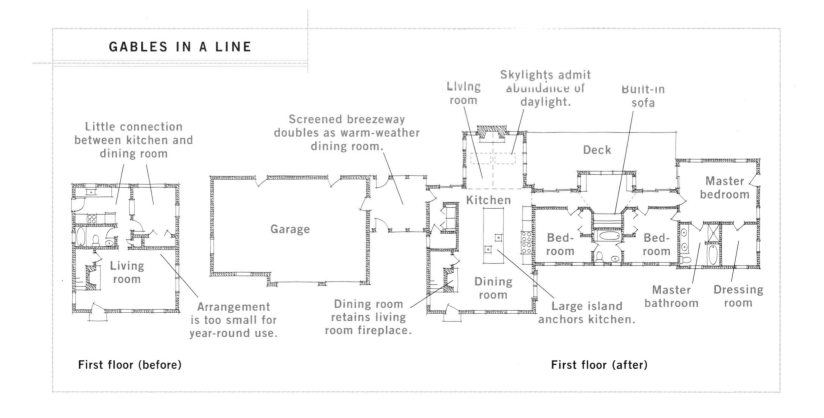

GABLES IN A LINE

Little connection between kitchen and dining room

Screened breezeway doubles as warm-weather dining room.

Skylights admit abundance of daylight.

Living room

Built-in sofa

Deck

Master bedroom

Kitchen

Bed-room

Bed-room

Garage

Living room

Dining room

Arrangement is too small for year-round use.

Dining room retains living room fireplace.

Large island anchors kitchen.

Master bathroom

Dressing room

First floor (before)

First floor (after)

The windows in the gable end of this house are typical Cape in their style and placement: two double-hungs below and two smaller windows above. The novelty is that they all grace a single bedroom.

doors, and trim—while sharing a gable roof of the same pitch. These similarities unify the house, so that it doesn't appear to be merely a collection of disparate parts.

Spare, crisp white trim was used to outline each component and help set it off from adjacent forms. Corner boards aren't necessary on a shingled house, but they help define this Cape. The wide **frieze board** does double-duty as both trim and the head casing above the windows; this was a matter of necessity, since the traditional low eaves didn't allow room for both.

ABOVE, **The prominent location** of the kitchen meant that the appliances and cabinets needed to be selected for looks as well as performance. The light-toned maple cabinets contrast with the cherry cabinets of the adjacent island.

LEFT, **When does an island** qualify as a continent? Two sinks on this extra-large island make it easy to share cooking and clean-up.

frieze board — A horizontal band of trim running under the soffit.

The breezeway between house and garage becomes a pleasant dining room in warm weather.

A Sensible Plan

One of the owners' peeves about the old house was that, with the living room's north-facing windows, the place could seem dreary on winter days. Because the renovated house was going to be used year round, it was important to rework the plan to admit more light to the interior.

Joe began by gutting the inside of the original house to create a large open room with a massive 4-ft. by 12-ft. island at its core. Joe built the island out of cherry and topped it with a concrete counter. The elevated end adds more storage and shields the view of dirty dishes from the new living room. This island alone offers as much counter space as an entire kitchen, and it was fitted with two sinks and two dishwashers. The former living room is now the new dining room. Its unconventional location, just inside the front door, makes sense for this gregarious family because so many of their gatherings happen to take place

How to Grow a House

BEFORE YOU JUMP feet first into a remodeling project, it helps to know the house—and yourself. If you are new to your Cape, you might want to live there a few seasons to get a better idea of the family's needs. The bay window you recently installed may be just where you'd like to add a den. A new wing of bedrooms might seem like an albatross if the kids are approaching college age. Should the redesign anticipate your decreasing mobility over the years ahead?

It's not easy—and sometimes not even pleasant—to forecast our personal futures. And yet families tend to grow and contract in patterns, and there's certainly some predictability to a person's physical changes. Architects have seen these scenarios unfold many times, and they can help you decide in which ways your house should grow. We all tend to think of our situations as unique, but a design professional may be able to spare you the fate of adding on rooms that will never see much use.

So much of family life takes place around the dining table. This one is prominently situated in front of the nearby fireplace.

around the dining table. The room's generous dimensions allow everyone to sit together at Thanksgiving and other seasonal celebrations. The existing fireplace adds some formality to the space.

The new living room extends to the south. With its vaulted ceiling, two skylights, and windows on three sides, this room now lets in an abundance of daylight in all seasons. There is no air-conditioning, but paddle fans and good cross-ventilation make the house comfortable even on the warmest summer days. The frame-and-panel treatment above the fireplace conceals a cabinet for the television set and matches the wall detail seen above the dining room's fireplace. The wide-plank pine

floors are new, but hearken back to the traditional flooring that would be found in an old Cape.

A hallway leads off the west side of the house, extending to the master bedroom. Along the way, it widens out to create a small sitting area that doubles as a library, with built-in bookcases and a comfy seat. In this location, the bench can serve as a retreat without the user feeling shut off from the rest of the house. Above the seat and bookcases is what appears to be a high window. In fact, this is an attic access door disguised as a window, with mirrored glazing (see the photo on p. 138).

Jo points out that a connecting door between the master bedroom and adjoining guest bedroom allows

With books behind and a view beyond, this sheltered spot is a natural place for quiet reading or a nap.

The massive kitchen island features cherry cabinets and a concrete countertop.

using the smaller room as either a nursery for a visiting grandchild or as a study. The master bedroom occupies its own little Cape at the end of the run and features a traditional window pattern on the gable wall. Collar ties above permit the ceiling to follow the underside of the rafters and to support light fixtures.

Chimneys of Legend

Chimneys are integral to our notion of what a traditional house should look like. And the bigger the house, the more chimneys we tend to think it should have. In line with that reasoning, this home is now crowned by four. There's one for the new fireplace in the living room,

The Run-On House

INSTEAD OF DESIGNING a single large addition that runs the risk of overwhelming or obliterating your Cape, it can help to visualize your home as an assemblage of distinct linking spaces. A good example is the interconnected farm buildings peculiar to colonial New England.

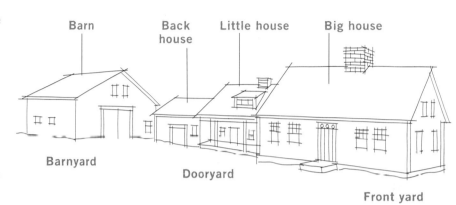

"Big house, little house, back house, barn," goes a traditional phrase that describes these distinctive structures. Each of the farm's four main sections had its purpose, its own degree of formality and a particular orientation to the property. Leaving the barn, you first went through the back house, where you could wash up before entering the kitchen in the little house. From the other direction, visitors could approach the main farmhouse (the big house) without walking through the barnyard.

The result is a house with a dynamic form—a complex of shapes that are visually more interesting than one large structure or several identical parts in a straight line. You can plan your house to have this appearance from the start, with an addition that looks as though it served the main house.

another for the original fireplace, and a third serving the furnace flue. The fourth chimney, above the master bedroom roof, is pure romance—Joe added it to help this section of the addition mirror the original Half Cape.

The visible tops of the chimneys look traditional but are in fact plywood boxes surrounding metal flues. Textured fiberglass was layered onto the plywood to mimic stucco and then painted white with a distinctive black "Tory stripe" that centuries ago marked the houses of New England loyalists.

Bill and Jo are happy with the transformation of their little beach getaway into a full-time house. For Joe, as well, the project clearly was something special. After the construction was completed, Joe was married in the house that he and his father had built.

Stone Sprawler

This covered walkway between house and garage frames the view to the shady garden while providing sheltered access to the back door.

ROBERT AND ELIZABETH WERE IMPRESSED BY their first glance of this stone New England Cape. The 2-acre parcel was landscaped with mature plantings, including a perimeter of coniferous trees that would ensure privacy all year round. Inside, they were struck by the home's "good bones," its classical trim, and the reasonably ample proportions of the rooms. But it was clear that the Cape would be too small for their family of five and that an expansion was imminent.

The house had been built in 1929, and it was well above the ordinary level of craftsmanship. Robert and Elizabeth enlisted the help of architect Jennifer Huestis to design an addition that would retain the hallmarks of the original Cape and avoid overwhelming its quaint scale. Their ambitions were sweeping. They wanted the house to admit more light and to take full advantage of the beautiful back gardens. There would be a bedroom for each child, a large breakfast room attached to a revamped kitchen, a mudroom, and a replacement for the tired garage.

The outline of most Capes is sketched in ruler-straight lines. The owners of this Cape preferred
the swooping roofline of an English cottage. The new brick chimney has precast concrete
"epaulets" as it steps up.

Small "eased" dormers are tucked down into the roof plane and have less of a presence than standard dormers. Copper snow guards at the eaves help prevent sliding snow from ripping off the gutters and dropping a drift onto the head of unsuspecting people below.

FITTING IN

Your Neighbor's Point of View

☆ **BE SENSITIVE** to your neighbors as you locate an addition. After all, your personal vision will be in someone else's view! It may help to walk around your yard and visualize the new addition from your neighbors' perspective. Will the addition block a cherished view? Will it throw their terrace into shadow? Note ways in which you can screen off your less-than-lovely elements—air-conditioning condensers, propane tanks, trash cans—from the view of others. A quick-growing hedge or vine-covered trellis may be the answer to maintaining good relations with the folks next door.

Embracing the Stone

The usual sort of addition is simply tacked on to the house: A family needs another two or three rooms, and the home sprouts a wing to accommodate them. Jennifer took a more sophisticated approach. Her design embraces the original Cape by wrapping in and around its stone walls, meshing the new with the old. Matching the existing stonework throughout would have been too costly, so instead the new work is sided with the white-painted shingles found on the residence's dormers. The contrast of stone and shingle breaks the Cape into smaller segments, helping it maintain a humble countenance, whereas a large, all-stone home might have seemed monumental. Also, the new large window openings were much easier to frame in wood than they would have been in walls of stone.

As with the original house, the addition is roofed with slate, an expensive alternative to asphalt shingles but one that should outlast virtually any other type of roof. The consistency in roofing material works to tie together the new and the old. The addition does add its own wrinkle, however, with its curved roofline. Elizabeth had always admired the swooping roofs of English Arts and Crafts homes, and in this project the curved silhouette gives the home a relaxed look that manages to avoid seeming at all stylized.

On this side of the Atlantic, Capes have had their own legacy of curved roofs. The influence of boat-builders could be seen in coastal homes, with roofs that resembled inverted ships' hulls; the gently curving rafters were formed from naturally bending trees, and they allowed a bit more headroom. Capes with these so-called rainbow roofs are now enjoying something of a revival for their distinctive look.

Taking advantage of the large lot, Jennifer designed the three-car garage as a separate building. Generally, it's easier to maintain the pleasing lines of a house if the garage can be treated as a traditional outbuilding. When the garage has to be an integral part of the house, there's the chance that its large doors will dominate the facade facing the street.

Although it connects the house and garage, the breezeway stands out as a structure in its own right, with its gable front and pilasters standing guard. The garage, its doors aimed to the side, has the scale and appointments of a small house rather than a place to hide the cars.

A Zoned Home

Three teenagers outnumber two parents, and the house is carefully zoned to segregate the grown-up formal spaces from the more relaxed family realm. The stone walls of the original construction help buffer the sound from room to room. A generous back hall, carved out of the former kitchen, serves as an in-between area amid these zones. From here, a new stairway runs up to the

A second stairway leads up to the children's bedrooms from the new back hall, providing a shortcut for the kids when they clatter downstairs for meals.

ABOVE, **The library,** formerly a slate-floored side porch, was fitted with cabinetry painted a refreshing blue. Its location, far from the family room, ensures that it remains a quiet retreat.

FACING PAGE, **This new hallway** offers the contrast of the home's original stone wall on one side and a translucent bank of windows on the other. The beckoning window seat has storage below.

children's bedrooms, while the house retains its more formal front stair.

In the new hall, as well as in other parts of the remodeling, you can still see the original stone facing; from the start, the architect and homeowners agreed to leave all these handsome walls in place and in full view. The finely executed woodwork looks all the more refined for its contrast with the rough, tactile surfaces of stone.

The ceilings in the original house were barely 8 ft. high. Jennifer wanted more height to build in the arches, pillars, and boxed beams you see here, and she chose the unusual strategy of dropping the floor in the family room and adjacent breakfast room and mudroom by roughly 1 ft. This guaranteed that the architectural effects wouldn't cramp the rooms.

The mudroom tends to be an unsung part of most houses, but this one is a favorite spot for Elizabeth because of the order it lends the household. Each of the five cupboards, with corresponding drawers below, is assigned to a family member. As long as the doors are

English limestone floors and a wall of glass elevate this mudroom to the status of a porch or sunroom. Each family member is assigned his or her own cupboard to stash coats, backpacks, and gear.

Substantial columns and a graceful arch span a traditional gateway between two rooms.

shut and the contents are hidden from view, the clutter is handsomely contained. The floor in the mudroom isn't just flagging from the nearby home center but English limestone, selected for the unusual mustardy color that complements the stone walls.

Putting the Kitchen in its Place

In the original floor plan, the kitchen was a throwback to an earlier era. It had been crammed into a dimly lit area with little room to maneuver and was little more than a utility room—off-limits to guests and not at all welcoming to family activities. Jennifer's design puts the kitchen where it belongs, alongside the back garden, with enough room to handle convivial gatherings. A large island can be used for both serving breakfast and

CONNECTING TO THE BACK GARDEN

This stone Cape seemed isolated from its sylvan surroundings. The new scheme incorporates a breezeway that permits easy access to the back garden; the new kitchen and breakfast room addition collects the views and daylight through banks of windows.

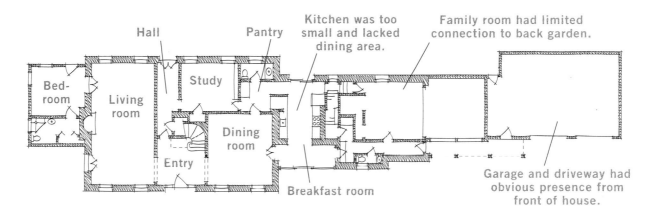

Hall Pantry

Kitchen was too small and lacked dining area.

Family room had limited connection to back garden.

Bed-room

Living room

Study

Dining room

Entry

Breakfast room

Garage and driveway had obvious presence from front of house.

First floor (before)

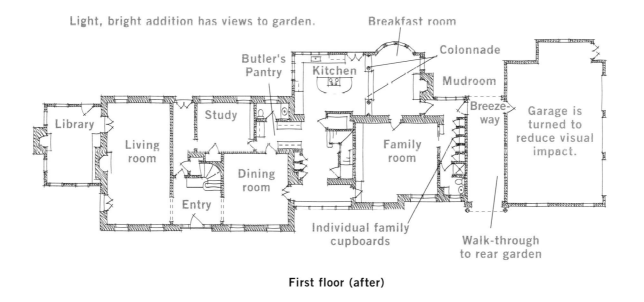

Light, bright addition has views to garden.

Breakfast room

Butler's Pantry

Kitchen

Colonnade

Mudroom

Library

Study

Living room

Dining room

Entry

Family room

Breeze-way

Garage is turned to reduce visual impact.

Individual family cupboards

Walk-through to rear garden

First floor (after)

setting out a buffet. A walk-in pantry off the back hall holds the bulk of the dry goods and reduces the need for wall cabinets in the kitchen proper. The white cabinets have the same understated sophistication as the woodwork elsewhere in the house, with a well-proportioned architectural solidity. The polished granite on the counters and backsplash was chosen for its similarity in color to the house's granite walls.

The breakfast room is set off from the kitchen by an arched colonnade incorporating bookshelves. The shal-

An advantage of a pantry is that the kitchen can have a wealth of windows instead of banks of wall cabinets.

low elliptical shape of the portal recalls the one at the breezeway, but here the columns are chubby and round and spring from the top of the shelves. The glossy paint, in the same hue as the walls, draws attention to their form. A breakfast room in name only, this elegant space is used for all but the most formal of meals. The fireplace has an English limestone hearth and surround, using the same stone as in the mudroom. A bay window graces the table with light. The facing stone wall was the outside of the original home, and the doorway into the family room is original as well.

The remodeling is characterized by this contrast of smooth and textured, heavy and weightless, opened up and concealed—and yet, from the outside, the house is very composed and serene. For many Cape owners, this is the goal: to transform the house without advertising the shape-shifting strategies within.

The former back door now connects the breakfast room and the family room. New millwork was painstakingly scribed around the surface of the original wall for a close fit between wood and stone.

The sturdy stone walls on this Cape suggest the home's connection to the earth.

CHAPTER FOUR

NEW HOMES FROM AN OLD PATTERN

ABOVE, **Old Capes sprouted** appendages over time and as families grew. This new Cape was built with the same room-size segments. The inset porch is a nontraditional convenience.

FACING PAGE, **It's easy to overwhelm** the straightforward, commonsense look of a Cape, and subtle effects seem to work best. These gable dormers are unusually low— they don't have side walls—so that they do little to interrupt the handsome simplicity of the style.

I F YOU ARE CONTEMPLATING A NEW CAPE, YOU can choose your own level of authenticity to the original New England style. You might want the house to be an exacting reproduction of a 1700s Cape. At the other extreme, you could go off on an architectural adventure, reworking the Cape's hallmark elements in a radical way. The most common course is to select certain classic Cape features for a balance of practicality and historical essence.

Whatever your take on a new Cape, you might want to ground your dreams of the perfect house with a visit to a few historic Capes. Photos and floor plans can tell you a lot, but there's no substitute for seeing these three-dimensional forms firsthand. Only then can you really appreciate the style's straightforward look and time-tested details.

Whether you look at houses in the flesh, in plans, or in photos, the challenge is to be influenced by what you see and yet remain open to concept-stretching

This house is new but borrows an old pattern of transom windows and trim in this reproduction of a historic front door arrangement. The light fixture is modeled after a coach light.

approaches. It's interesting to look at the photo of the house in "The Fundamental Cape" (below) that's believed to be New England's oldest example and then to examine the modern interpretation shown with it. You can see the family resemblance—the ways in which many of the original ideas have weathered the storms of fashion and industrialization to appear here in an evolved form.

An Architecture of Substance

It's not all that difficult to take the Cape's external details—dormers, trim, shutters, multipaned windows—and sprinkle them over a box to end up with something that looks vaguely like a New England–flavored home. But this haphazard assemblage of ingredients tends to yield a mediocre result, as no doubt you've seen from driving past the plain facades in suburban

retro guide

☆ The Fundamental Cape

THESE TWO CAPES, built nearly 350 years apart, are clearly cut from the same cloth. Compare the overall size and shape, the **fenestration,** the center brick chimney, and the low-to-the-ground stance.

With the current interest in a return to smaller houses, Capes continue to offer the twin economies of price and scale. And they do so in a quaintly traditional way that manages to avoid being bland. They key element may be the steeply pitched roof, which in our culture seems to be a universal symbol of sanctuary. That distinctive silhouette remains an icon of home sweet home, despite the somewhat fleeting popularity of Modern and Ranch houses.

fenestration ⌐ The arrangement of windows and doors in a structure.

subdivisions. You can't just costume a cube with nostalgic parts and expect the result to hold together visually.

A better approach is to design a new house from the inside out—to consider the house as a three-dimensional volume instead of as a structure on which to super-impose cute features. You don't have to duplicate the "four rooms down and two rooms up" pattern of old Capes. Instead, respond to your local climate, the slope of the site, views that shouldn't be shut out, the appearance of the surrounding houses, and your need for specific spaces. Only when factors like these begin to shape your thinking should you figure how everything will come together within that distinctively shaped form.

Especially in a relatively diminutive Cape, care should be taken to use space wisely rather than lavish it on formal rooms that are rarely occupied. Architect Sarah Susanka stresses the value of including an "away room," a place out of the hubbub of activity but still connected to it *visually*. In allowing individual family members some distance from the fray, the house will seem larger. Sarah suggests using glass doors between this private space and an adjoining family room, both for a measure of acoustic privacy and to prevent a feeling of isolation. To ensure that the away room isn't just used on special occasions, it can be furnished with the stuff of everyday life—desks, comfy chairs, books, and a stereo system. If it's as austere as a waiting room, you can't expect family members to hang out there.

TWENTY-FIRST-CENTURY ROOMS

In designing a new Cape or rebuilding one from the ground up, you'll likely want to add rooms that weren't found in postwar houses, much less in the Colonial originals. Just as Royal Barry Wills needed to integrate indoor plumbing into his 1930s adaptation of the early Cape, today's designers may need to allocate a room, or

This expanded Cape takes the form of two houses, with the entry door between them. By breaking down a home into sections, you can have plenty of space without creating a structure that overwhelms the property or the neighborhood.

at least a corner, to a computer and its gaggle of related hardware. Beyond that, you may want to plan for a home office, from which to run an in-home business or merely the business of the home.

Give special consideration to where the office will be within the layout, thinking in terms of privacy, quiet, and access to an entrance. Even a small office alcove will need souped-up electrical and communication lines to handle all the devices we rely on—and the easiest time to add them is during construction.

Managing a household's affairs can demand a personal computer, files, bookshelves, and plenty of quiet. The best spot for a home office is in a relatively isolated part of the house, if you are fortunate enough to have such a space.

Cape Shape

A Cape's steep roof is not just the lid on a living space but also an emblem of the style. As the previous chapters have shown, the roof molds the shape of the second-floor rooms tucked under its rafters. This level can be left unfinished as an attic, but bedrooms and baths can take on an especially homey quality when nestled under sloped ceiling planes—and in fact these spaces are one of the best-loved features of the Cape.

Because of the low, head-ducking nature of the space, you'll probably want to consider gaining height and admitting more light with dormers. It's interesting to note that dormers are one elaboration that can *contribute* to a Cape's pedigree look rather than detract from it. And while they were usually added some years after construction, your new Cape can have them from

The exposed underside of the floor above gives this kitchen a warm, rustic ceiling. An open ceiling like this requires that extra thought be given to running electrical lines discretely to lighting fixtures.

A wraparound porch was added to this Cape to help shield it from winter weather,
giving it something of a farmhouse look.

A Window Glossary

☆ **JUST AS EYES** are the windows to the soul, windows express the soul of a home. Here are the basic types you'll be most likely to choose from.

Awnings are outward-swinging windows that hinge at the top. They operate with a crank or a push-out lever. In a rainstorm, awning windows help direct the water away from the opening below.

Casement windows swing out on side hinges, like a door, and are operated by a crank or a lever. They are a good choice for use over a kitchen counter; they introduce a lot of fresh air because they can be opened so wide.

Double-hung windows are the type most commonly used in Capes. They consist of two operable sashes that slide within independent tracks. Only half of the area of the window can be open at a time. Double-hung windows are often flanked by shutters, but this convention isn't found in all traditional houses.

Bay windows are found in many modern Capes. These are angled projections with windows in each of the three facets. The box bay window is similar; it looks like a pushed-out picture window with solid sides.

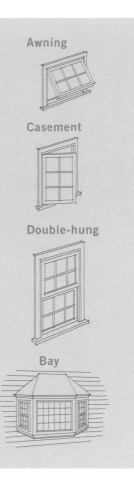

Awning

Casement

Double-hung

Bay

Three small awning windows dance up the side of the gable, paralleling the stairway's upward path within.

simulated divided light ⌐ A window that uses a grille to make a large pane of glass look as though it were divided into smaller units.

true divided light ⌐ A window with individual panes held withina grid of muntins.

the start. By including them as part of the roof's framing, you spare yourself the effort and expense of cutting through the roof to retrofit them at a later date.

WINDOWS WITH CHARACTER

The windows of early Capes had many individual panes because of the small standard sizes of glass shipped over from England. These panes typically were used in a pattern of four wide and two or more high, in both of a

LEFT, **The windows** of the bathroom dormers are set low, allowing the dormers to have a lower profile. You have to look hard to spot the skylight between them.

BELOW, **A shed dormer** can increase the head height over a substantial area of the top floor. Here, the dormer allows the upstairs hall to be run along an exterior wall.

double-hung window's sashes. In specifying the windows for a new Cape, you aren't restrained by these size limitations, of course. And in addition to double-hung units, you can choose from casements, awnings, fixed-sash windows, bays, and skylights. Whatever your preferences, you may want to stick to the convention of **true divided light** windows, or **simulated divided lights** with fixed grilles that look like the real thing. Windows with removable interior grilles don't look quite as authentic, but they are

less expensive and have the advantage of making the glass easier to clean.

In locating windows on your Cape, give some thought to challenging the rigid symmetry of the historic model. By building new, you have the luxury of coordinating the placement of furniture and fixtures with the window positions. Still, the exterior will be more pleasing if the windows relate to each other in some way. A random arrangement won't be as effective. No matter that the mind may want novelty, the *eye* likes seeing pattern, groupings, and alignment.

SHUTTERS, REAL AND PRETEND

Some of the distinctive features we like about Capes, inside and out, are vestigial elements that have become more ornament than anything else. We no longer have to shutter our windows against storms or heat with logs in a drafty fireplace. These features have become as outdated as buggy whips and antimacassars. But architectural throwbacks can still elicit a warm, settled feeling,

ABOVE, **In a renovation,** you can use a basic traditional element such as a divided-light window in novel ways. In the bathroom, they're placed one on top of the other to make good use of the available space.

RIGHT, **Real, operable shutters** look a lot more convincing, especially when sized for the window they adorn. These frame-and-panel shutters feature snappy cutouts of a gaff-rigged sloop, appropriate to a Cape along the Atlantic Coast.

Three divided-light windows placed side by side allow wall space for the headboard below.

adding character to what might otherwise seem to be a no-fun, cost-conscious series of practical decisions.

Installing shutters isn't a mandatory part of building even a tradition-inspired home. Not all older homes had them, although this seems to be the popular conception. If you do go to the trouble and expense of including shutters, it's best to do it right. These fixtures should be hung on either side of a single double-hung window, and from hinges attached to the face of the jamb casing. Avoid embellishing a wide window with skimpy shutters that couldn't possibly cover the opening, and stay away from plastic shutters that are nailed or screwed directly to the wall.

The Benefit of a Budget

Beyond selecting the color for siding and trim, the roof is another large expanse that should be considered in the palette for the exterior. The red roof on this house is a reference to the region's Scandinavian population and the typical roof color of their traditional homes.

C HANCES ARE THIS ISN'T YOUR HEADACHE, BUT designing a new house with unlimited funds can be intimidating—the possibilities are so endless as to be hobbling. A strict budget, on the other hand, may act as a constraint that helps keep the focus on what is most important to our daily lives.

When architect Eric Lewtas designed a home for his family on a gently sloping New Hampshire lot, he had the benefit—and the challenge—of making ends meet. That meant paring down the wish list to the essential of living areas, work spaces, and bedrooms. It also meant giving up a few luxuries, like a fireplace and a formal dining room. There were a couple of requirements: a screened porch that would be used for as many weeks as the New Hampshire summer would allow and a separate garage with plenty of storage. Because this was an owner-designed project, it may have benefited from Eric's extra care. But when hiring a design professional, you should expect this same level of attention to interesting details and clever uses of materials.

The orientation and configuration of a house and a detached garage introduces a
third space: the outside area that is defined between the two buildings. This is the
dooryard, the traditional place where household chores were done, and is a different
spot altogether from a more formal front yard.

Dipping Into the Past

To bring this Cape out of the ordinary, Eric drew on Scandinavian homes for the red roof, and he took inspiration from the family's last home, a Bungalow, for such hallmarks as exposed **rafter tails,** tapered porch posts, and cottage-style ganged windows.

As suits its location in New Hampshire, the house is clad in both clapboard and shingles. Clapboard girdles the bottom portion of the house, while shingles set off the second-story floor line above. There are a couple of unexpected shifts along the way. The second-story shingles have a slight flare along their lower edge, with the practical function of helping shield the clapboard below from the dripping rain. There is a bump-out that allows space for the entryway and a sunny extension of the kitchen that the family calls the "day room." A small boxed bay, with its own little roof and exposed rafter tails, recalls similar features on Bungalows; the rafter tails are cut with a decorative swoop, and reach beyond the edge of the roof to form a shallow *brise soleil,* or sun screen, visible from the window.

As with older Capes that made good use of the sun for light and heat, a long wall of this home faces due south. The sun's path follows the pattern of Eric and his wife Winnie's daily routine. In the morning, the eastern sun streams into the kitchen area. The midday sun warms the house through front-facing windows. By the end of the day, late afternoon light reaches into the living room to greet the family's return from work or school.

The floor plan was designed for the long interior views that can help to make a house seem larger than it is. But this isn't an interior entirely without walls and doors. Before reaching the core of the house, people have to pass through a vestibule with doors at either end, an important energy-conserving feature at this

This Cape picked up a few tricks from a later style: the Bungalow. There are two siding materials, two siding colors, a slight kick at the lower shingle courses, and exposed rafter tails on the entry roof.

rafter tails ⁓ The lower ends of rafters, which are left exposed in some architectural styles to contribute to a simple, countrified look.

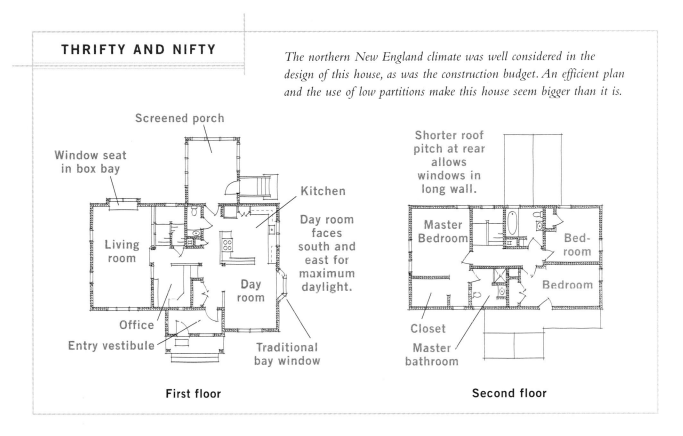

The northern New England climate was well considered in the design of this house, as was the construction budget. An efficient plan and the use of low partitions make this house seem bigger than it is.

Screened porch

Window seat in box bay

Kitchen

Day room faces south and east for maximum daylight.

Living room

Day room

Office

Entry vestibule

Traditional bay window

First floor

Shorter roof pitch at rear allows windows in long wall.

Master Bedroom

Bed-room

Bedroom

Closet

Master bathroom

Second floor

northern latitude. Since the garage is separate from the house, the vestibule provides the principal place to kick off snowy boots before coming inside.

Using Partial Walls

Once inside, the first floor is revealed completely. Eric used low walls to define the edges of spaces without cutting off views; they also mark the boundaries of the kitchen proper and the corral-like office. The low walls are clad in painted medium-density fiberboard (MDF) beadboard to distinguish them further from the surrounding drywall.

In this open plan, the kitchen functions like an old-fashioned keeping room, with cooking, eating, and family activities all rolled into one informal rectangular space. Here, Winnie and Eric can cook and chat and keep an eye on the little ones. The kitchen affords a direct line of sight into the home office and the living room beyond, making this house ideal for hosting casual parties.

This grille permits the muddy drips from snow boots to drizzle down through the decking. Although this house is in snowy New Hampshire, the idea would work equally well for sandy feet trooping home from the beach.

The cooking center in this open kitchen is contained behind a low beadboard partition. The wall cabinet doors suggest the typical Bungalow window's pattern of a multipaned sash over a single-light sash.

The living room is large, extending front to back and taking advantage of views down the hill to a rolling meadow. It is one step lower than the rest of the house to allow higher ceilings, a feature that helps set the room apart as something special. The living room includes a window seat in its boxed-out window bay, offering a spot to curl up and read.

The back porch, with double-hung windows on three sides, might also be called the sunroom. In the summer, with window screens in place, the porch is kept cool by cross-breezes and its northern exposure. The high ceiling promotes a chimney effect, drawing hot air up and out of a gable-end louver.

After sundown, dimmable ceiling fixtures turn the box bay window into what appears to be a lantern from the outside. The bay's rafter tails are ornamented with a delicately swooping cut.

Foundation Fundamentals

THE FOUNDATIONS OF the earliest Capes were merely heavy wood timbers that kept the floor-boards a few inches off the sandy or soggy ground. These houses could be moved by dragging them across the dunes on wooden skids. Later on, houses in permanent settlements were built over a stone basement.

Most modern Capes have a foundation of concrete poured into wooden forms or of precast concrete blocks. To resist the heaving force of frozen soil, the foundation walls must extend down into the earth to below the frost line, the depth to which the soil can be expected heave with the effects of freezing. Frost lines vary from region to region, and foundations may extend many feet below the ground in Maine but only inches in Florida. A full foundation forms a habitable basement, but many postwar Capes were of slab-on-grade construction, in which the home's lowest level is a poured concrete pad at ground level.

A well-crafted stairway can be too attractive a feature to hide behind flanking walls or in a back hall.

miter cuts ⟶ A saw cut made at an angle, often a tricky procedure where moldings meet at corners.

Because this window seat is on the north side of the house, it admits even and diffuse light all day long.

Eric trimmed the rooms with details he and Winnie had enjoyed in their previous home. He used plain fir stock with a natural finish that brings out this inexpensive wood's attractive honey color. The head casing over the windows and doors runs past the side casings to avoid having to make time-consuming **miter cuts** at the joints. This is the sort of simple, honest design that distinguishes Bungalow interiors.

This Bungalow ethic—using readily available materials in a straightforward way—allowed Eric to construct a relatively inexpensive home that nevertheless is graced by his custom touches. There is none of the applied ornamentation that builders often resort to in trying to justify a higher price. A need to economize can be a real help in making aesthetically sound decisions.

Inexpensive off-the-shelf, single-glazed windows encircle this unheated porch. In the summer, the lower sashes are raised all around to open the room to breezes.

Little "a" Architecture

ABOVE, **An advantage** of the Cape's characteristic low stance is that porches and decks can be linked to the yard with few steps and no handrails.

FACING PAGE, **The more sides a porch** has, the better it will be able to take advantage of breezes. This porch wraps around the house for maximum cooling and superior views.

A NEW HOME DOESN'T HAVE TO DRAW ATTENTION to itself. And that may be preferable on a site that itself is stunning. This Cape guesthouse, designed by architect Peter Zimmerman, sits in a bowl-shaped hollow on a peninsula with wide views of Chesapeake Bay. It is modeled on the Cape form and aesthetic, and because the style has a long association with the coast, the structure fits in gracefully on this mid-Atlantic shoreline.

There were some construction limitations because of the house's proximity to the water; environmental regulations required that it sit directly on the foundations of a cabin that had been torn down to make way for the new project. Although this would seem confining for an architect, Peter found that rebuilding on the footprint of the cabin helped him arrive at a design that suggested the house was really quite old.

Cape Chronicle

Exterior trim details suggest the notion that the house had expanded over the years. The portion that appears to be the original core is in the classic Cape form, with the quintessential silhouette: center masonry chimney

and simple steeply pitched gable roof. Stone from the former cabin and several outbuildings was salvaged for the new fireplace and chimney. Two small dormers, centrally located on either side of the roof, look as though they had been added at a later date, reinforcing the sense that the house has a history. The cedar clapboard siding was finished with a semitransparent wood stain so it looks as if it had been weathered by many storms.

Another apparent step in the "evolution" of this house was the addition of the wraparound porch. Note how the clapboards at the sides of the porch roof come to an end at the corner boards of the central house—it's as if the porch were added at a later date. Even the kitchen seems to be enclosed within a former back porch. You can see the suggestion of porch posts in the facade of the house by the outdoor shower enclosure.

This snug bedroom niche adds another meaning to being tucked in at night. The window on the left peers down into the dining space. It can be shuttered for privacy and quiet.

FACING PAGE, **A two-story space** invites groups to be convivial, and this house does see occasional large and loud gatherings. The bleached look of the wood-clad walls and ceiling—not to mention the trophy fish—establishes a coastal theme.

RIGHT, **Even without painted** surfaces, the mixture of wood tones in this house adds depth, color, and variation to the interior. The color comes from the surrounding landscape of sky, sea, and lawn.

The herd of rafter tails above the outdoor
shower is a reflection of the owners'
passion for horses.

An Expansive Cape

Indoors, the plan is compact enough that one or two
people can be comfortable using the house as a weekend getaway. And yet the porches allow the little house
to stretch and accommodate large parties. The interior
walls and ceilings are sheathed with knotty pine boards
that were lightly stained to suggest age. The dining room
is open to the underside of the roof, with a ceiling of
rough-sawn pine boards. In contrast, the sitting area feels
cozier with its ceiling of conventional height, exposed
joists, and built-ins to either side of the fireplace.

The wraparound porch keeps harsh midday sunlight
from coming in the French doors that ring these spaces.
The doors have transom windows that "pull some texture from the outside," as Peter puts its, allowing the

Functioning Fireplaces

☆ **A CENTRAL HEATING SYSTEM** rates high in convenience but
scores close to zero on the ambience scale. A fireplace, although
a somewhat messy and inefficient feature, can serve as the
home's symbolic center even when there isn't a fire blazing
within. And it certainly suits a Cape interior.

The rooms of early Capes were dominated by their large fireplaces, which were responsible for warming the family, cooking
dinner, and lighting the interior. A single massive brick chimney
might have a cluster of fireplaces at the base, one for each
room. In the keeping room's fireplace, a fire burned all year
round for cooking food and baking bread in a built-in oven.

The easiest way to add a fireplace to a newer Cape is to build it along an outside wall
of the living room or family room. You'll be in for a lot more work if you choose instead to
install the fireplace along an interior wall, because of everything involved in excavating
and in tying the chimney into the roofing system.

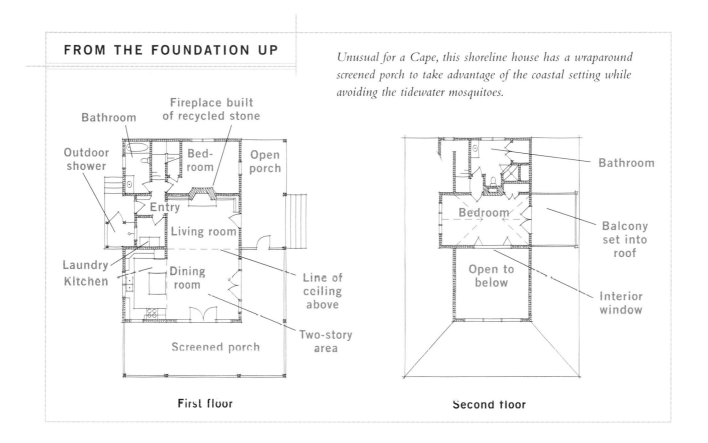

FROM THE FOUNDATION UP

Unusual for a Cape, this shoreline house has a wraparound screened porch to take advantage of the coastal setting while avoiding the tidewater mosquitoes.

Bathroom

Fireplace built of recycled stone

Outdoor shower

Bed-room

Open porch

Entry

Living room

Laundry Kitchen

Dining room

Line of ceiling above

Two-story area

Screened porch

First floor

Bathroom

Bedroom

Balcony set into roof

Open to below

Interior window

Second floor

porch's cedar ceiling to be viewed from within. The transoms also add to the visual height of the doors, helping bring the eye upward into the double-height volume.

The one bedroom on the second floor has interesting ceiling planes formed by the dormers. An interior window looks down into the dining space below, making this a destination for grandchildren who want to spy on the grown-ups. The bedroom has its own balcony overlooking the water; its railing design is a nod to the Chippendale themes that were once popular throughout the region. The diagonals of these balusters are echoed by the cross-bucks of the storage-area doors under the porch. This house is an excellent example of how you can go beyond merely working from historically flavored plans. Because we expect that houses will grow over time, it's possible to give the impression of age by designing what appear to be added or modified sections. A few inexpensive details is all it takes to suggest the legacy of past owners—while you, the fortunate first owner, have complete control over the project.

The bedroom balcony is tucked within the form of the porch roof. Similar in spirit to the exposed rafter tails of the porch, the dormer displays the ends of ornamental beams at its peak and eaves.

A Cape with a New Twist

ABOVE, **This north-facing porch** shelters the front door from the elements. Its roof is cut away to accommodate double-hung windows for the second-floor bathroom and hallway.

FACING PAGE, **The second-floor porch** resembles the prow of a ship. The cut-away corners and jutting alcoves provide views in a remarkable number of directions.

FRED AND LINDA LIVED ON AN ISLAND OFF THE coast of Rhode Island for 30 years, eyeing the handsome older houses in their neighborhood. When a nearby lot came on the market, they decided to build their own custom-designed home with the help of architect William Burgin, using shingles, steep roof pitches, and the kind of porches that are part of the New England vernacular.

The long, thin lot limited the overall form the house could take. And there would be no fudging of setbacks here, because Fred happened to serve as both the zoning enforcement officer and the building inspector for the town.

The Hit List

Fred and Linda gave William a list of more than a dozen must-haves for their new house. Several of these were the usual things architects hear: 2,000 sq. ft. of living space, two-car garage, and two or three bedrooms. One request that stood out was that there would be a free-flowing floor plan that didn't distinguish between formal and informal spaces. In this community of 6,000 year-round residents, formality is left behind on the mainland. The couple also wanted a place for

LEFT, **On the second floor,** this private nook of a porch is reached through the home office. The untreated red cedar shingles will slowly weather to a silver gray.

BELOW, **Dynamic angles** and a variety of window sizes animate this house's visage. The architect took off on a geometric adventure, cutting into and adding onto the traditional Cape form.

The fireplace nook's adjacent window seat offers a dog's-eye view in a sunny bump-out. Floors are fir, reclaimed from beams that were purchased at a lumber salvage operation.

Zoning In

BEFORE JUMPING FEET FIRST into any new project, visit your local municipal offices for zoning regulations. Here are some of the terms you're apt to run into:

Property lines are the legal limits of your plot of land, but there are other invisible lines to be concerned with.

Setbacks are the minimum distances your proposed structure can be placed from the property's edge, establishing your required yards: front, sides, and back.

Lot coverage concerns the percentage of the lot that your house's footprint (or roof area) occupies. Zoning codes may include decks, pools, terraces, and drive-

ways as lot coverage, so read the local requirements carefully before planning a large deck or addition. If Capes in postwar developments predate current zoning codes, they already may be the maximum legal width for the lot, so that any expansion has either to go out the back or up into a full second story.

In some communities, zoning laws limit the number of **stories,** or levels. The basement may be considered a story, depending on how deeply it is set in the ground. The level beneath the steeply pitched roof of a Cape is usually counted as a story as well.

ABOVE, **The unusual** angled walls create long diagonal views through the house, making it seem larger than it is. You almost have the sense of being able to see around corners.

LEFT, **Winders were used** instead of an intermediate landing, allowing the overall run of the stairway to be shortened. The triangular stairwell opening is formed by the angled twists of the plan's overlaid rectangles.

Linda's baby grand piano, a window seat for Molly the dog, and generous second-floor spaces that wouldn't look as though they were stuffed into "pigeon dormers," as Fred calls the undersize versions.

Beyond these requirements, Fred and Linda were also attracted to the notion of building something unusual, rather than a predictable box. In his profession, Fred had inspected plenty of both ordinary houses and extraordinary ones, and he appreciated the ways in which architects can come up with novel approaches to shelter.

In a conventional house, designed with right angles and vertical walls, the second floor is extruded directly up from the one below, with aligned exterior walls and interior partitions. This is the simplest and most economic way to build a structure. Instead, William Burgin twisted

two classic Cape forms in a way that defies the norm, creating a house that seems to be in constant motion.

The drawings show how a standard rectangular floor plan was overlaid with another such plan at a 45-degree angle. Where the second floor tucks in, the first floor protrudes. Some interior partitions follow the parallel sides of that floor's rectangle, whereas others are free to form intriguingly shaped areas. The home unfolds in origami fashion, but rather than creating pinched corners where dust mice tend to breed, this angled strategy has led to useful alcoves for the stairwell, powder room, and sitting nook in the living room. The second floor includes a triangular "tree house" porch that extends out over a lower porch to capture views to the south and the sea beyond.

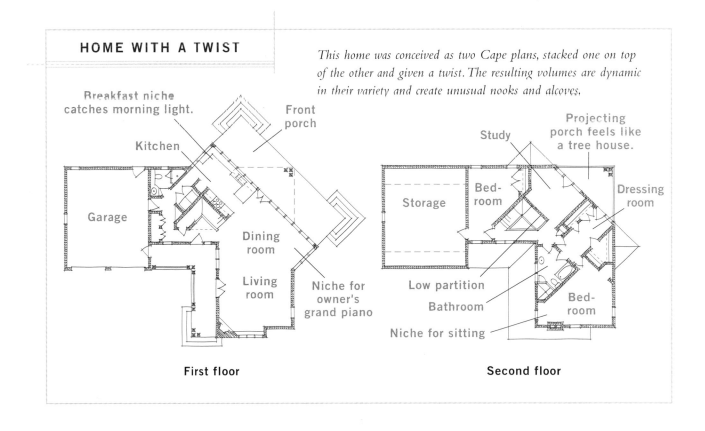

HOME WITH A TWIST

This home was conceived as two Cape plans, stacked one on top of the other and given a twist. The resulting volumes are dynamic in their variety and create unusual nooks and alcoves.

Breakfast niche catches morning light.

Front porch

Kitchen

Garage

Dining room

Living room

Niche for owner's grand piano

First floor

Study

Projecting porch feels like a tree house.

Storage

Bed-room

Dressing room

Low partition

Bathroom

Bed-room

Niche for sitting

Second floor

Another result of this strategy is that the house has more exterior facades than you'd find in the typical home, adding opportunities for windows and capturing twice the views. On the inside, all these angles and views create the illusion of a larger home.

Domestic Virtues

You might expect this house, with all its twists and turns, to seem cockeyed or difficult to furnish. In fact that hasn't been the case. As bold as the architect's conception may be, there are inviting spaces throughout the home. For example, a breakfast table and window benches were tucked in the kitchen's projecting south-facing corner, making this the next-best spot for morning coffee (the second-floor porch being Fred's first choice).

With any project on a limited budget, you have to allow yourself some atmosphere-garnishing luxuries to balance out your frugal selections. You might prefer cedar roofing but go with asphalt shingles to save enough money to upgrade the trimwork. In this house, inexpensive cabinets were painted on site to allow splurging on honed Zimbabwe granite countertops and custom-made backsplash tile.

Although you can't see it from the photos, this house was designed to be as weathertight and energy efficient as possible. It is **superinsulated,** with considerably more fiberglass insulation than required by the building code. There was no skimping on the windows either. They have insulated glass and are designed for high wind speeds, a necessary precaution where hurricanes are not uncommon. The door hardware was also selected for use near the sea, because ordinary fittings tend to corrode.

The house has five heating zones, programmable to regulate temperatures in tune with Fred and Linda's schedule. This means that the unoccupied spaces aren't heated, with a considerable energy saving. The bedrooms are comfortably cool during the wee hours, and the kitchen is toasty by the time the couple sits down to breakfast. Once Linda and Bill are off at work, the house cools down again—until just before dinnertime, when the heat comes on for a cozy evening at home.

Fred built this house himself, working weekends for 16 months. He now has a lot more empathy for the contractors whose work he inspects. "It's a lot easier to inspect a house than to build one to code," he says.

superinsulated — An unusually high level of insulation within a building.

The kitchen features a breathing backsplash, in which tiny awning windows are squeezed into the narrow space.

In the typical Cape configuration, windows are set in from the corners and spaced evenly. In this rule-bending house, a sunny corner is invested with rows of double-hungs just above the kitchen banquette.

A Cape Reborn

ABOVE, **Old casement windows** that were salvaged during demolition found new use in the bedroom.

FACING PAGE, **Interior windows** look down into this two-story space, forming an atrium effect.

I F AN OLD HOUSE IS REALLY FAR GONE, REBUILDING can be as ambitious as starting from scratch. Architect Robert Knight and his wife, Lucia, had lived in their 1790s Cape for several years and raised a family before getting up the resolve to do what was necessary—strip away the effects of 200 years' worth of deferred maintenance.

Any last vestiges of quaintness had long been lost—restoring the house to museum quality was never a practical option. Thus the project began by reducing the structure to its bare bones. Plaster ceilings and walls, floorboards, and floor joists all came away to reveal the underlying timber-frame structure.

The frame established the thick, volume-defining lines that guided the rebirth. The builders had to make repairs to a couple of rotten posts, but for the most part the framing was intact, a testament to the craftsmanship and materials of the era. A first step in the home's new life was to wire brush and oil the frame until it gleamed like a piece of furniture.

Although Robert and Lucia conceived the new arrangement, Dominic Mercadante, an architect in Robert's office, did the actual design work. The primary intents were to introduce more light into the downstairs

A beamed ceiling, if left open to the floor above, tends to allows dust and dirt to filter down through the floorboards— not a happy state of affairs when the lower room is a kitchen. The area between the joists can be filled in to avoid the problem.

and to make it seem spacious. As with most houses of this vintage, the windows had been few and small and the rooms seemed dim and shadowy. And, while the living area within the frame was fairly generous, much of it had been devoted inefficiently to back halls and a laundry.

Working with a Skeleton

The new floor plan eliminated a ramshackle vestibule and mudroom on the first floor, reconfigured the stairway to the second floor, and created a dramatic two-story space instead of re-establishing one of the

second-floor bedrooms. Even after subtracting this bedroom, the house still offers 1,750 sq. ft. of living space.

The old front door to the house was done away with in favor of a less formal entry into the 4-ft. bump-out of the kitchen. The roof over this little addition is a continuation of the main roof slope, keeping the clean lines of the Cape. Why bring people directly into the kitchen, the heart of this home? This flies in the face of architectural convention. But this kitchen, although a work center, has welcoming appointments, and the feeling is not at all cold or institutional. It has new wide-plank pine floors, installed with the square-head

This antique Cape was heading toward its demise when the owner stripped it down to the post-and-beam framing and built a bright new house. The two-story dining room is now the focus, and windows have been used liberally to fill the rooms with light.

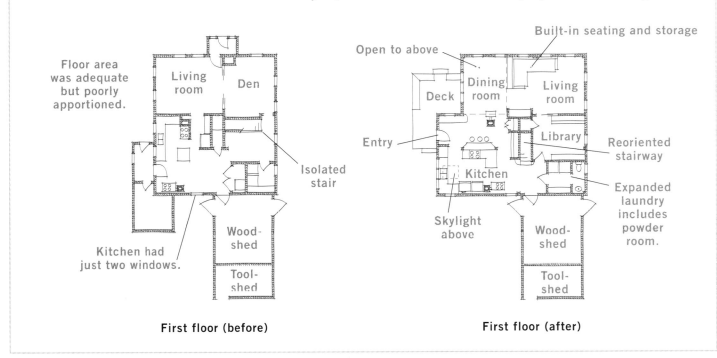

First floor (before)

First floor (after)

nails used for the original remaining floors. And a warm-hued variety of granite known as Texas Rose was used for a countertop, along with butcher block and plastic laminate. A glass-fronted hutch just inside the front door lends a certain formality to the entry.

Once inside, visitors are drawn toward the light flooding into the two-story dining area. This generous space was made possible by the large dimensions of the original Cape; a postwar Cape of the Levittown variety wouldn't have afforded the same opportunity. Robert added windows along one gable end of the house, forming a gallery for artwork in between the openings. A high window acts something like a skylight, providing a look at the treetops and letting in additional daylight from a lofty angle. Old windows were salvaged from the original house and set into *interior* walls for views from the bedrooms down through the two-story area.

Timber Framing

TO BUILD a truly traditional Cape, begin with a traditional frame—a system of massive timbers measuring 6 in. or 8 in. across. The frame isn't merely nailed together, as with today's speedy stud-wall construction. Instead, the timbers are joined with mortise-and-tenon and other joints that don't rely on metal fasteners. This construction technique requires special skills, but it continues to be used, not only for sturdiness but also because of the inherent drama and beauty it brings to a room. Early timber framing was typically of oak, but fast-growing, relatively inexpensive softwoods are now often used instead.

Managing the Views within the Home

Beyond the dining area is a living space defined by its lower ceiling and a built-in combination of a sofa and sideboard. As seen in other houses featured in this book, the boundaries between rooms can be suggested by variations in ceiling height and floor level, without the constricting effect of walls.

There are many views within the house itself, across spaces both horizontally and vertically—from the dining area up to the overlook at the second-floor hallway and from the largest bedroom back down through the salvaged windows. In Maine, the summers are fleeting and daylight is especially precious, and bright interior finishes help make the most of the light. White-painted walls, trim, and ceilings set off the dark wood of the timbers. There is one remaining joist spanning the dining

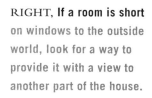

ABOVE, **Modern appliances** need a roosting spot in every kitchen, whether reclaimed or new. Here, the microwave sits companionably near the cookbooks.

RIGHT, **If a room is short** on windows to the outside world, look for a way to provide it with a view to another part of the house.

RIGHT, **This Cape stands** up to a snowfall with its steeply pitched roof and prominent chimneys. Contentment radiates out from the windows.

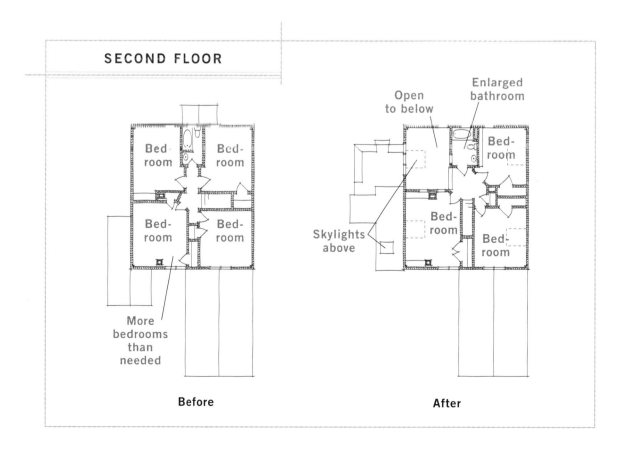

SECOND FLOOR

Bed-room

Bed-room

Bed-room

Bed-room

More bedrooms than needed

Before

Open to below

Enlarged bathroom

Bed-room

Bed-room

Bed-room

Skylights above

After

area, defining where the floor above had been and providing a place to hang overhead lighting.

The house is heated in the winter solely by two wood-burning stoves, one in the kitchen and the other at the entrance to the dining room. The heated air moves up to the bedrooms by convection. A fan circulates the warmth through ductwork into the library, which is the only enclosed room on the first floor, other than the laundry.

Although this house was inspired by its 200-year-old frame, the majority of the construction is new, and the house works so well that Robert and Lucia offer the plans in their catalog of small house designs. They've experienced firsthand that the layout lends itself to modern living while retaining the flavor of the Colonial era.

Built-in furnishings are an efficient way to pack seating, storage, and display into a small area. Designing them as part of the architecture ensures that they complement the house.

The roofline of this Cape has been extended to create an unobtrusive shelter for the new entry. Small barn sash windows are a traditional way of bringing in light to a low second floor.

To the Edge and Back

ABOVE, **Bay windows** don't have to make a display of themselves. With trim that matches the house and an extension of the home's roof pitch, this bay changes the interior far more than it does the facade.

FACING PAGE, **With no intervening wall,** the vista through the living spaces is punctuated only by the chimney.

S ANDRA, THE OWNER OF THIS REBUILT CAPE, had a sandy problem—the home originally was located on an eroding Cape Cod dune and would have been lost to the sea if she didn't have it moved inland. She faced a second challenge, posed by local building codes. If she chose to renovate the house, the floor area could be increased by no more than 20 percent and the original materials and overall form had to be retained.

Architect John Bryer was resourceful in getting around what appeared to be daunting problems. To obey the spirit of the law, he took apart the walls and set them aside carefully for reuse, a traditional form of recycling known as *flaking*. The wall components were loaded onto trucks and moved back 100 ft. to a new foundation. To deal with the square footage limitations, John incorporated the area that had been occupied by the rickety old tool shed and garage.

Recasting the Remains

In the process, a motley collection of low rooms was transformed into an airy, light-filled, year-round house. John's design makes the most of the available volume within the walls and beneath the rafters, so that the

The scrubby Atlantic coastline, with cranberry bogs beyond, is the setting for this Cape, which was rebuilt from the walls of an existing house.

house retains its distinctive beachy Cape feel—and stays within the code limits. The shifting roof and wall planes at the front and back elevations of the house subtly signal the hierarchy of spaces within. The result is a small compound of Cape-shaped units, most of them joined together and one standing alone in the landscape.

The plan offers large central living spaces with bedrooms at the extremities. To ensure a view out across the adjacent cranberry bogs from every spot, the rooms are arranged in a line along a light-filled corridor.

The guest bedroom is detached from the house, sitting in its own pavilion. This room enjoys plenty of privacy and forms one side of the sheltered courtyard deck. Its cluster of windows facing the sea is ornamented with arching trim at the top, as are the clerestory windows facing the walkway. Although the guest room is new, the effect is that of an outbuilding that has been converted to living space, helping the home to seem as though it has been on its site for decades.

Trellises are normally reserved for outdoor use, but by introducing them indoors they can reinforce a home's connection to the landscape. This house links the outdoor cedar trellis, visible at the end of the hall, to the corridor's overhead grille, made of a somewhat more refined wood, cherry. The natural light streaming through skylights along the ceiling calls attention to this effect.

The art studio is a well-lit room, with a bay window that fits unobtrusively into the facade; its roof is simply an extension of the main roof's slope, and the detailing is decidedly unfussy. As elsewhere in the house, the ceiling plane follows the lines of the roof, helping ensure that the home's modest-size spaces don't feel cramped.

White trim is used not only to border the guest room pavilion but also to form an arch above the clerestory windows.

ON THE EDGE

This Cape was teetering on the brink—it was precariously close to the receding dunes. The house was dismantled, and much of the original material was used in re-creating the building 100 ft. inland.

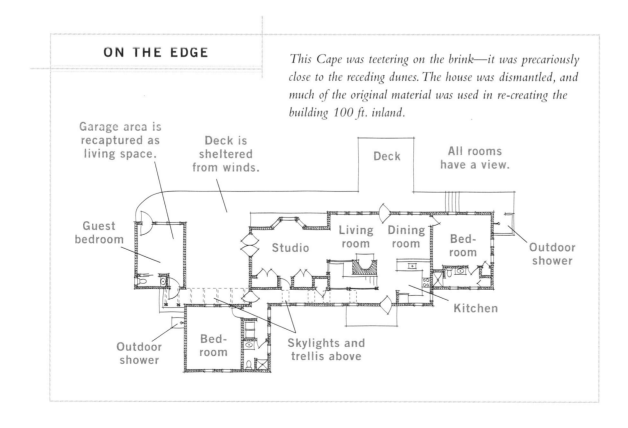

Garage area is recaptured as living space.

Deck is sheltered from winds.

Deck

All rooms have a view.

Guest bedroom

Studio

Living room

Dining room

Bed-room

Outdoor shower

Outdoor shower

Bed-room

Skylights and trellis above

Kitchen

Hallways tend to be dark matters of convenience. This passageway is brilliantly lit by skylights and a bank of windows. The trelliswork overhead adds interest to the ceiling, and its cross-bars visually shorten the hall-way's run.

Using Fir and Fireplaces for Warmth

Wood surfaces are an ideal counterpoint to plentiful white walls. Both end walls of this house are clad in Douglas fir, a species that is usually used for framing. Its pronounced, lively grain makes a decorative feature out of these surfaces.

A pair of stacked fireplaces anchor an open stairway leading from the living room to the playroom below. They provide a focal point when the evening darkness lies beyond the curtainless windows. The fireplaces were constructed of brick and then painted white; they offer ledges on which to display Sandra's artwork. The hearth of the upper fireplace is raised to place its crackling flames closer to eye level for people seated on the sofa.

A finished basement seems an unlikely element in a beach house, but the code restrictions suggested making

ABOVE, **A low, windswept land-scape seems** to call for a house that hugs the earth, as Capes have in their indigenous environment for over 300 years.

LEFT, **If you've got** a stunning view, flaunt it. A bay window, with glazing aimed in three directions, creates a panorama as well as bringing in a lot of daylight.

Thinking Environmentally

☆ **WHEN CONTEMPLATING** a new Cape or restoring an old one, consider its impact on the natural environment, especially if your property has wetlands, is near water, or is on the beach. Check for special restrictions that are specific to the site before beginning the design process. During the construction period, you may be required to erect a temporary fence to prevent debris and runoff from affecting the surroundings.

Remember that old Capes, like most old houses, have layers of paint that contain lead. Paint scrapings must be gathered and disposed of with care so that the lead doesn't leach into the groundwater or accumulate in the surrounding soil. Contact your local health department for responsible ways of dealing with this toxin.

The open-riser stair, with hefty treads spanning the stringers, is a modern adaptation of a traditional Cape stair that climbs alongside the chimney stack.

use of this option for more space. The open stairway wraps around the fireplace in traditional Cape fashion, but it leads down to the bright playroom rather than up to an attic. Daylight finds its way down to this level through the skylights in the hallway above.

This house reaches out to the landscape with an intriguingly shaped deck. All too often, a deck is nothing more than a rectangular stage attached to the house, but this one winds along the ocean facade, extends raft-like out into the cranberry bogs, and then meanders back into a sunny outdoor room sheltered on three sides by the house's walls.

In this new location, with its new configuration, the home's snug grouping of forms is suited to the wind-sculpted site. The traditional vocabulary of weathered shingles and white trim ensures that the house looks at home on the stretch of sandy land that gave the style its name.

The predominately pale interior scheme of this house is carried out in the painted brick, walls, and ceiling and the lightly bleached floor. The wood tones of the kitchen and trellis beyond offer an agreeable contrast.

CHAPTER FIVE

NEW DIRECTIONS

ABOVE, **The pergola over** the entrance courtyard is befitting of a Nantucket cottage, and it helps tie this California house to an earlier tradition from clear across the country.

FACING PAGE, **The roof overhang** of this house on the Cape recedes at certain places around the deck, permitting the glass doors to have transom windows.

"I F AN ARCHITECT FROM MARS WERE TO TAKE a cross-country jaunt along the old Grand Army highway, now U.S. Route 6, starting in lush, semi-tropical California and ending in the sandy, windswept hook of Cape Cod, 70 miles out in the Atlantic Ocean, he would be struck by the persistence, throughout his journey, of one particular building type…the Cape Cod cottage."

Although these words were penned in 1949 by the editors of *Architectural Forum* magazine, they could just as well have been written today. And there is no reason to think that the statement couldn't be made 50 years from now. The Cape's recurring popularity is a testament to its pleasing lines and quiet efficiency. Long after it evolved in the Colonial era, the Cape returned as a desirable style in the early 1900s, then figured prominently in the postwar building boom. And now Capes seem made to order for the recent trend of building smaller, rationally sized homes that have strongly traditional elements.

CALIFORNIA BAYSIDE CAPE

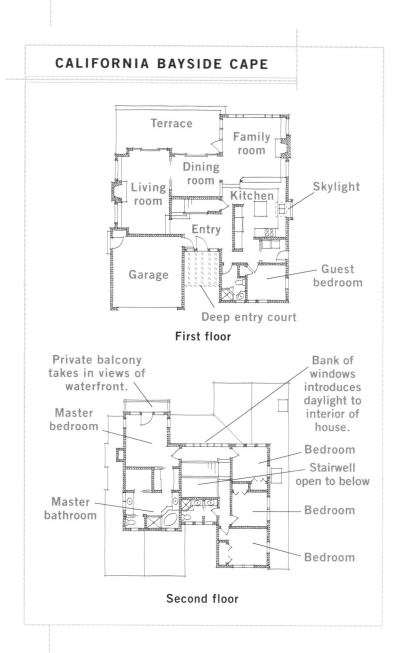

Terrace

Family room

Dining room

Living room

Kitchen

Skylight

Entry

Garage

Guest bedroom

Deep entry court

First floor

Private balcony takes in views of waterfront.

Bank of windows introduces daylight to interior of house.

Master bedroom

Bedroom

Stairwell open to below

Master bathroom

Bedroom

Bedroom

Second floor

Traditionally, Capes put little emphasis on the stairs—they were just a way of going from one floor to the other. By presenting a stairway from the side instead of head on, you can turn it into a feature, as was done to show off this balustrade.

This isn't to say that the latest round of Capes is restricted by acknowledging the past. The two homes featured in this chapter are part of the Cape's ongoing legacy—drawing on historic pattern, materials, and shapes without being at all trite or predictable. Each house has gone in a fresh direction while staying in touch with its distant origins.

In the Image of a Cape

This California house, designed by architect Colleen Mahoney for Cindy and Jim, draws on the East Coast for its inspiration. Cindy recalled her childhood summers on the Massachusetts island of Nantucket, and asked that Colleen come up with a home that referred to the region's Capes.

This California house reaches out to its seaside site with large expanses of glass and a balcony off the master bedroom. The Cape influence can be seen in the crisp white trim that outlines the windows and roof.

The new house is stacked two stories tall to fit a lot of living space into a narrow site. At first, the result doesn't much resemble a Cape. But as with the Capes toured in chapter 4, this home is composed of room-size components that suggest it might have grown over the years, in response to the needs of a succession of families. You can see what appear to be modest additions and a shed dormer across the back. Once you step inside, however, you know you're in a contemporary structure—the bold, open plan and use of windows

make that clear. So, while the incremental look of the exterior softens any raw, new edges the home might have, the spaces within are cut loose from historical precedent.

The choices of colors, materials, and smaller design elements also contribute a traditional flavor. There is a refinement about these details that sets the house apart from much modern construction. Generous, strongly graphic white trim contrasts with gray shingles. There are divided-light windows throughout—on awnings,

In contemporary homes, kitchens are often open to family spaces, an expanded role that suggests bringing the cabinets up to the level of fine furniture. This kitchen treats the person on scullery duty to both a window with a view and a skylight overhead.

the upper sashes of double-hungs, and in the French doors. Approaching the house, you pass through a trellis-like fence and under a pergola that straddles the front entry court, elements that were conceived as part of the overall design.

As with other family-oriented houses in this book, the informal areas are open to each other. The living room, dining room, and family room are all arranged at the back of the house, with easy access to the terrace—a world away from the constraining floor plans of the past. Through the medium of a receptive architect, the owners' way of life has shaped the space.

The divided-light clerestory windows refer to houses of the past, and they help tie the very contemporary interior with the somewhat traditional facade.

The Cape's customary form has been tweaked, incorporating eccentric roof shapes that wrap around the traditional steeply pitched gable of the center portion. The house sits well with the scrubby coastal landscape.

Upside-Down Cape

Back on Cape Cod, architect Jeremiah Eck was asked by Allan and Linda to design a house suited to the blustery shoreline setting. The lot slopes down to the water, and Jeremiah adapted to the change in elevation with a floor plan that reverses the roles of home's two levels. Four bedrooms are located on the lower floor, so that the master suite and living spaces can make the most of the spectacular view from the level above. Modern steel-pipe railings at the balustrades of the wraparound walkway and deck are decidedly nautical and contemporary, as is the spiral stair leading "below deck." But the silhouette of the home seems very much in the Cape tradition—this is a structure that has adapted to its environment, rather than lording over it.

Jeremiah designed the street face of the house to be very contained and private, with minimal windows that

suggest a certain reserve. In marked contrast, the elevation looking out over the sea is pierced with an array of windows, not one of them a double-hung unit. In addition to fixed glass panels and skylights, the fenestration includes casements, awnings, and sliders.

Yet the house retains the elements of the vernacular style, with weather-silvered shingles, wide window trim, a steeply pitched roof, and a tall chimney at the center of it all. In keeping with the Cape heritage, the roof has minimal overhangs—with two exceptions. At the front, the pitch curves to cover the entryway, and at the rear another extension shelters the sliding doors that lead out to the deck.

Indoors, you can spot several features borrowed from traditional Capes; but as on the exterior, the familiar is given a twist. Or a *curve,* in the case of the living room ceiling, which recalls the early bowed roof (or rainbow roof) of Capes particular to this region. Locals were accustomed to building ships' hulls and applied the same techniques when raising roofs. The curved rafters have greater strength and allow more headroom, as well as contributing a nautical look. The ceiling is finished with cedar planking, which also recalls ship construction.

The fireplace core is as prominent as it would be in a vintage Cape. Its solid white mass separates the kitchen from the living room, and hearths serve both sides. Again in Cape fashion, a steeply pitched stair, almost ladder-like with its open risers, ascends to the loft tucked under the steep roof.

The planked ceiling is an abstraction of the rainbow roof built over early Cape houses. The windows at the end of the room follow the curve and frame the rising sun.

From this view, you can see the arched shape of the roof over the living hall and the way it interlocks with the pitched roof slopes. The protruding bay under the curved roof contains the dining area.

ABOVE, **The ladder-like stairway,** made of the same materials as the deck railing, has open risers that make it transparent to daylight.

FACING PAGE, **The exposed steel** framing that supports the loft is a modern version of the exposed post-and-beam skeleton of a historic Cape.

The Essence of Home

The Cape Cod house is an enduring American icon that comes in many regional flavors. In this book, we've looked at Capes that recalled English Cotswold cottages, Capes with postmodern overtones, Capes that are rich in detail and materials, and Capes that make do with plainer parts. We've seen Capes transformed into Bungalows and Colonials, and Ranches that have morphed into Capes.

As I review this collection of houses, I am impressed anew that they are linked as much by a common spirit as by a family resemblance. Across the centuries and across the continent, this legacy remains unbroken. It is no less vital for being intangible, for having an essence that even New England architects can't quite put their drafting pencils on.

COMING HOME TO THE CAPE

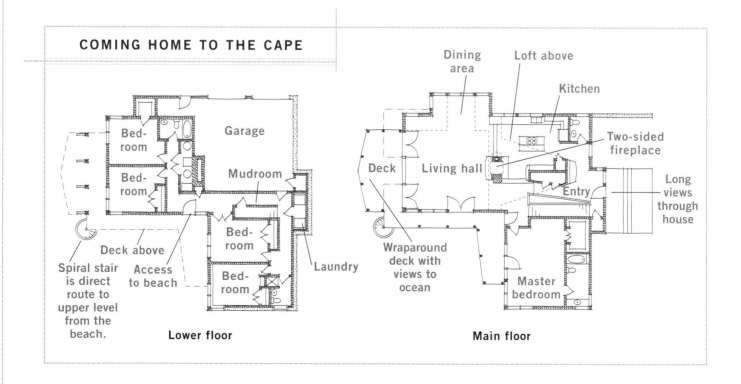

Lower floor

Bedroom
Bedroom
Garage
Mudroom
Bedroom
Bedroom
Laundry
Deck above
Spiral stair is direct route to upper level from the beach.
Access to beach

Main floor

Dining area
Loft above
Kitchen
Two-sided fireplace
Deck
Living hall
Long views through house
Entry
Wraparound deck with views to ocean
Master bedroom

Sources

HISTORIC INFORMATION

Plimouth Plantation
P.O. Box 1620
Plymouth, MA 02360
508-746-1622
www.plimoth.org/ppinc.html
This replica of the original 1627 Pilgrim colony is a living history museum that has more than a dozen homes on view.

Colonial Williamsburg
Williamsburg, Virginia
1-800-HISTORY
www.history.org
The 173 acres and more than 500 restored and reconstructed buildings of the historic section of Williamsburg, Virginia, bring the pre-Revolutionary period to life.

Falmouth Historical Society Museum
55-65 Palmer Ave.
Falmouth, MA 02540
508-548-4857
This Cape Cod museum features two restored homes dating from the early nineteenth century.

Old Sturbridge Village
1 Old Sturbridge Village Rd.
Sturbridge, MA 01566
508-347-3362
www.osv.org
The 1830s come to life in this open-air folk museum, consisting of a collection of historic buildings and artifacts and staffed by costumed villagers and farmers.

Mystic Seaport
P.O. Box 6000
75 Greenmanville Ave.
Mystic, CT 06355
860-572-0711
www.mysticseaport.com
This bustling nineteenth-century village and shipyard hosts year-round activities.

Levittown Public Library
1 Bluegrass Ln.
Levittown, NY 11756
516-731-5728
www.nassaulibrary.org/levtown/
The Levittown History Collection includes photos, newspaper articles, and other materials relating to the development of this historic twentieth-century suburb.

Society for the Preservation of New England Antiquities
141 Cambridge St.
Boston, MA 02114
617-227-3956
www.spnea.org
A wealth of information on older buildings is available from this important institution. Their Web site offers links to other organizations, sources, and related publications.

Historic American Buildings
Survey/Historic American Engineering Record
HABS/HAER collections
www.loc.gov/rr/print/145_habs.html
Measured drawings, photographs, and data sheets documenting works of American architecture and engineering at the Library of Congress.

BOOKS

Baisly, Clair. *Cape Cod Architecture.* Orleans, MA: Parnassus, 1989.

Burton, Virginia Lee. *The Little House.* Boston: Houghton Mifflin, 1942. Copyright renewed 1969.

Cummings, Abbott Lowell. *The Framed Houses of Massachusetts Bay 1625–1725.* Cambridge, MA: Harvard University Press, 1979.

Dwight, Timothy. *Travels in New England and New York.* New Haven, CT: Author, 1822.

Hubka, Thomas C. *Big House, Little House, Back House, Barn.* Hanover, NH: University Press of New England, 1984.

Hunter, Christine. *Ranches, Rowhouses & Railroad Flats. American Homes: How They Shape Our Landscapes and Neighborhoods.* New York: Norton, 1999.

Jackson, Kenneth T. *Crabgrass Frontier: The Suburbanization of the United States.* New York: Oxford University Press, 1985.

Kelly, Barbara M. *Expanding the American Dream: Building and Rebuilding Levittown.* Albany, NY: State University of New York, 1993.

Kelly, J. Frederick. *The Early Domestic Architecture of Connecticut.* New Haven, CT: Yale University Press, 1924. Reprinted by Dover, 1963.

McAlester, Virginia and McAlester, Lee. *A Field Guide to American Houses.* New York: Knopf, 1984.

Peters, Frazier Forman. *Pour Yourself a House.* New York: McGraw-Hill, 1949.

Poor, Alfred Easton. *Colonial Architecture of Cape Cod, Nantucket, and Martha's Vineyard.* New York: Dover, 1932.

Rybczynski, Witold. *Home: A Short History of an Idea.* New York: Viking, 1986.

Schuler, Stanley. *The Cape Cod House: America's Most Popular Home.* West Chester, PA: Schiffer, 1982.

Schuler, Stanley. *Saltbox and Cape Cod Houses.* West Chester, PA: Schiffer, 1988.

Sleeper, Catharine and Sleeper, Harold R. *The House for You to Build, Buy or Rent.* New York: Wiley, 1948.

Susanka, Sarah with Obolensky, Kira. *The Not So Big House: A Blueprint for the Way We Really Live.* Newton, CT: Taunton, 1998.

Wills, Richard. *Houses for Good Living.* Stamford, CT: Architectural Book Publishing, 1993.

Wills, Royal Barry. *Better Houses for Budgeteers.* New York: Architectural Book Publishing, 1941.

Wills, Royal Barry. *Planning Your Home Wisely!* New York: Watts, 1946.

MAGAZINES

The Cape Cod Cottage, Part 1. Architectural Forum, 90, no. 2 (Feb. 1949): 88–94.

The Cape Cod Cottage, Part 2. Architectural Forum, 90, no. 3 (Mar. 1949): 100–106.

FEATURED ARCHITECTS

Arcus Design Group (p. v)
418 Eagle View Blvd.
Exton, PA 19341
610-458-9900

David Beckwith & the Beckwith Group
(pp. 27 bottom, 94, 96, 97)
P.O. Box 1226
1380-B Route 44
Pleasant Valley, NY 12569
845-635-9315

Jay Warren Bright, AIA
(pp. 5, 35, 88 bottom, 89)
65 Elm St.
West Haven, CT 06516
203-776-0798

Bryer Architects (pp. 45 bottom, 198–205)
160 Second St.
Cambridge, MA 02142
617-354-2360

William Burgin Architects (pp. 182–189)
150 Bellevue Ave.
Newport, RI 02840
401-847-3339

Robert Cardello Architects
(pp. 10–17, 43, 100 bottom)
97 Washington St.
South Norwalk, CT 06854
203-853-2524

Caswell Daitch Architects (pp. 78–85)
9604 Bruce Dr.
Silver Spring, MD 20901
301-585-8360

Tucker Chase Architect (pp. 102–107)
88 Academy Hill Terrace
Stratford, CT 06615
203-375-1093

Edmund Clemente (pp. 29, 88 top, 98 top)
327 Birch Rd.
Fairfield, CT 06430
203-254-1060

Gary deWolf Architects
(pp. 92, 98 bottom, 108–115, 166 top, 167)
319 Peck St.
New Haven, CT 06513
203-776-2194

Jeremiah Eck Architects (pp. 207, 212–215)
560 Harrison Ave.
Suite 403
Boston, MA 02118
617-367-9696

J. E. Elliott Architect (pp. 6 bottom, 162 top)
5127 Bonham Rd.
Oxford, OH 45056
513-523-2552

Robert Gerloff Residential Architects
(pp. 52–59)
4007 Sheridan Ave. S
Minneapolis, MN 55410
612-927-5913

Mark R. Halstead Architect (p. 42)
1295 Norman St.
Bridgeport, CT 06604
203-335-8448

Huestis/Tucker Architects (pp. 148–157)
2349 Whitney Ave.
New Haven, CT 06518
203-248-007

Knight Associates Architects (pp. 190–197)
Beech Hill Rd.
Blue Hill, ME 04614
207-374-2845

Joseph B. Lanza Design and Construction
(pp. 4, 6 top, 18, 33, 41 top, 138–147, 158, 160,
164, 166 bottom)
511 Bay Rd.
Duxbury, MA 02332
781-934-5720

Eric Lewtas Architect (pp. 168–175)
32 Pickering Farm Rd.
Hancock, NH 03449
603-525-9408

Mahoney Architects (pp. 7, 206, 208–211)
P.O. Box 1053
Tiburon, CA 94920
415-435-6677

Mahoney Architects (pp. 116–123)
70 Seven Star Ln.
Concord, MA 01742
978-287-4223

Mary Meagher Design (p. 161)
45 Narragansett Ave.
Jamestown, RI 02835
401-423-0882

Jeffrey S. Rubin, AIA, Architect
(pp. 36, 41 bottom)
4833 Del Ray Ave.
Bethesda, MD 20814
301-654-8886

SALA Architects (p. 87)
440 Second St.
Excelsior, MN 55331
952-380-4817

Scot P. Samuelson, AIA-NCARB
(pp. 30 bottom, 37, 100 top, 101, 165 top)
P.O. Box 766
Old Lyme, CT 06371
860-434-7767

Spitzmiller and Norris
(pp. 21, 60–69, 70–77, 91 top)
Suite 206, Building 1
5825 Glenridge Dr.
Atlanta, GA 30328
404-843-3874

Tancredi Spano Architects (p. 86)
210 Marble Ave.
Pleasantville, NY 10570
914-741-1086

Thunder Mill Design (pp. 22, 45 top, 95 top)
5 Winter St.
Montpelier, VT 05602
802-223-3112

Tunney Associates Architects & Designers
(pp. 38 top, 90, 165 bottom)
306 Pine Orchard Rd.
Killingworth, CT 06419
860-663-2019

VELOCIPEDE Architects (p. 38 bottom)
5270B University Way NE
Seattle, WA 98105
206-529-9356

WESKETCH Architects (pp. 124–131)
1932 Long Hill Rd.
Millington, NJ 07946
908-647-8200

Royal Barry Wills Architects
(pp. 9, 25, 40, 95 bottom)
8 Newbury St.
Boston, MA 02116
617-266-5225

Z: Architecture (pp. 46–51, 131–137)
61 Jesup Rd.
Westport, CT 06880
203-227-8433

Peter Zimmerman Architects (pp. 176–181)
828 Old Lancaster Rd.
Berwyn, PA 19312
610-647-6970

Index

Index note: page references in italics indicate photographs; references in bold indicate illustrations.

A

Arbors, 68, *69*, *80*, *82*, *98*, 100
Attics, 44–45, 52–59

B

Balustrades, *60*, 62, *76*
Basements, 44
Bathrooms, *38*, 38–40, *40*, *56*, 56, 67, 82, *106*, 106, *154*
Beadboard, 14, 15, *67*, *103*
Bedrooms, *212*
    dormer, *22*, *43*, 54–56, *56*, *181*, 181
    kid's, *131*, 131
    master, 55, *55*, *66*, *142*, 147
Bench, 50, *51*, *95*
Board-and-batten, *65*, 65
Breakfast rooms, 63–65, *64*, 120, 155–57, *157*
Building codes, 68, 185

C

Cabinets, kitchen, *105*, *143*, *172*
Capes
    appeal, charm of, 4–8
    economy of, 6–7, 18–19
    hallmarks of, 18–24
    renaissance of, 25–30
    sizes of, **23**
Ceilings, 84–85, *213*
    beadboard, *15*, *64*, 65
    beamed, *66*, *192*
    second floor, *43*, *122*, *123*, *181*, 181
    tin, 120–22, *121*
Chimneys, 22, *147*, *149*, 198, *199*
Collar ties, 54–55, *55*
Colonnade, 62, 63
Columns, 82, *83*, *97*, *116*, *117*, 119, *155*, *156*
Cornice, 102
Cross gable, 63
Cupolas, *127*, 128, *128*

D

Decks, *80*, 81, 100, 113–14, *115*, *141*, *206*, *207*
Dining rooms, 7, *74*, 75, 77, *77*, *84*, 85, *112*, *144*, 144–45, 179, *180*
Dormers, *4*, *45*, 162–64
    adding, 36, *80*, 82, *122*, 122, *123*

gable, **44**, *159*
Nantucket, 14–15, *16*, *17*, **44**
shed, **44**, 108, *109*, *118*, *164*
variety of, *29*, *118*, *150*

E

Entryways, 10, 68, *98*, *195*
Environment, integrating, 68, *69*, 72, *72*, 81, *204*, 204
Exterior materials, 134–35, *168*, *170*

F

Family rooms, *21*, 120, 128, *129*, *136*, 137
Fences/gates, 72, *73*, 78, 83, 137
Fenestration, 160
Fireplaces, 12, 19–23, *94*, *140*, *145*, 157, *157*, *178*, 178, *185*, 202, *205*
Floor plans
    addition, **10**, **41**, **63**, **92**, **105**, **111**, **119**
    expansive remodel, **126**, **128**, **135**, **141**, **155**
    new house, **171**, **179**, **187**, **208**, **214**
    rebuilt home, **193**, **194**, **201**
    reworked, **48**, **75**, **81**
    second floor, **17**, **54**, **66**, **105**, **113**, **120**
Floors, 27, 40, *64*, 65, *140*
Foundations, *173*, 173
French doors, 81, 99, *102*, 106, 130, *131*
Frieze board, 141, 143

G

Garages, 151, *169*

H

Hallways, 12, *124*, *132*, 152, *153*, *202*
Historic capes, *4*, *5*, *8*, 18, 20, *24*, 24–30, 32, *88*, 160

I

Islands, **76**, *110*, *143*

K

Kitchens, *27*, *134*, *143*, 144
    as family space, 37–38, 120–22, 135–37, *210*
    lighting, 70, *71*, 122, *162*
    open, *12*, 12–14, 34, *35*, *39*, *121*, 124, *125*, *172*, 210
    reworked, *38*, 50–51, *51*,

75–76, *105*, 106, *110*, 127–28, 154–55
    windows, *39*, *65*, 70

L

Landscape, *67*, 68, *69*, 81, 137
Levittown, 24, *24*, 28, 97, 114
Lighting, natural, 58, 98–99, *202*, *203*
Living rooms, 12, 14–15, 20, 24–25, 29, *41*, *211*
Location, location, location, 10, 83

M

Miter cuts, 174
Moldings, **57**, *107*
Muntins, 17

N

New capes, 158–67
    architectural overview, 160–61
    budget-based, 168–75
    California bayside, 206–10
    inconspicuous, 176–81
    from old, 190–97, 198–205
    shapes of, 162–67
    with a twist, 182–89
    upside down, 210–15
Nursery, 81–82

P

Playrooms, 14, *14*, 16
Porches, 100, 105–06
    back, *45*, 45, *111*, 173–74, *175*, 184
    front, *36*, 102, *103*, *104*, 108, *109*, 116–19, *118*, 130, *130*, *176*, *182*, *183*
    screened, *98*, 100
    wrap-around, 176, *177*, 178, 179, *179*
Portals, *49*, 49, *155*, 155
Portico, **10**, 12

Q

Quarter-sawn, 49

R

Rafter tails, 170, *178*, *179*
Remodels, 10–17, *11–17*, 60–69, 70–77, 78–85, 116–23
    added story, 52–59, 65–66, 86, *91*, 92–94, *93*, 102–07, *104*
    expansive, 124–31, *127*, 132–37, 138–47, 148–57
    into other styles, 95–98, 102–07, 108–15

strategy/planning, 30–34, 40, 86–91, 144, 146, 147, 151, 185
Renovation/Restoration/Reproduction, 90
Ridge, 12
Roofs
    gambrel, 8, *9*, 18, *93*
    hip, 102
    pitch of, **19**, *18*, 19, 102–05, 160, *203*, *212*, 212
    varieties of, 18, *28*, *149*, 150, *151*, *168*, *195*, *212*, *213*
Rooms, clustered, 20–23

S

Showers/tubs, 28, *28*, *29*, 67
Shutters, *165*, 166–67
Six-over-one, 46
Skylights, 58, *123*, *124*, 126, *134*, *140*, 145, *164*, *202*, 204
Soffit, 119
Stairways, 58, *58*, 77, *151*, 152, *174*, *186*, *204*, *208*, *214*
Stick framing, 94
Stone, 148, *149*, 150–51, 152, *153*, *157*
Storage, *80*
    built-in, 34, *45*, 50, *56*, *91*, *140*
    built-in book, 12, 52, *53*, *59*, *146*, *152*, *162*, *196*
    closets, *124*
Sunrooms, 14, *15*, *16*, *30*, 82, *83*, *89*, 91, *95*, 99
Superinsulated, 188

T

Timber framing, 193
Trim, *6*, 14, 19–20, **20**, 78, *79*, *107*, 143, *157*, *201*

W

Windows
    adding, *10*, *26*, 36, *156*
    arch-top, *54*, 55
    awning, 17, *165*, *166*, *167*, 188
    bay, 36, *39*, 165, *173*, *198*, *203*
    casement, *16*, 17, 70, *71*, *121*, 165
    double-hung, 17, *142*, 165, *189*
    multipaned, *4*, *172*
    simulated divided light, 165
    transom, 16, 179–81, 206, *207*
    true divided light, 164, 165, *166*, 173
Window seats, 58, *59*, 152, *153*, *173*, *185*, *189*, *203*